25 Myths You've Got to Avoid— If You Want to Manage Your Money Right

The New Rules for Financial Success

Jonathan Clements

Simon & Schuster

For Hannah and Henry

SIMON & SCHUSTER
Rockefeller Center
1230 Avenue of the Americas
New York, NY 10020

SIMON & SCHUSTER and colophon are registered trademarks
of Simon & Schuster Inc.

Designed by Levavi & Levavi

Manufactured in the United States of America

10 9 8 7 6 5 4 3

Library of Congress Cataloging-in-Publication Data
Clements, Jonathan.
   25 myths you've got to avoid if you want to manage your money right: the
new rules for financial success / Jonathan Clements.
     p.   cm.
   Includes index.
   1. Finance, Personal.   I. Title.
HG179.C6512   1998
332.024—dc21   97-30430
                                                          CIP

ISBN 0-684-83982-2

ACKNOWLEDGMENTS_____

Many ideas in this book got their first airing in my Tuesday column in *The Wall Street Journal*. The "Getting Going" column would never have been launched or have thrived but for the support of Barney Calame, Dan Hertzberg, Glynn Mapes, Gay Miller, Paul Steiger and especially Fred Wiegold. My thanks.

The book itself also benefited from much support and encouragement. Financial experts John Cammack, Kenneth Klegon, Ross Levin and Eric Tyson kindly reviewed the manuscript. So too did a fistful of friends, family members and colleagues, including Richard Clements, June Dosik, Richard Dosik, Devra Golbe, Tom Herman, Tony Kitslaar and Fred Wiegold. My mother, father and mother-in-law even found their way into the manuscript. Mom, Dad, Sally, you see those barbed comments? The editor slipped them in when I wasn't looking. Really.

I never would have embarked on this project but for the urging of Wes Neff, literary agent extraordinaire. And the manuscript would never have been finished but for Fred Hills, my editor at Simon & Schuster.

The burden of the book's progress, however, was borne most heavily by Molly, my partner in grime. For eight months, you lived with this book, from the 5:00 A.M. alarm to the evening collapse. It wasn't so bad, right? Maybe you shouldn't answer that.

The dedication? That goes to my two glorious children, Hannah and Henry, for no good reason, except that you are indeed glorious. No, you didn't help with this book. But your occasional silence was golden.

CONTENTS

INTRODUCTION: HOW YESTERDAY'S RULES
BECAME TODAY'S MYTHS   11

MYTH NO. 1:   YOU CAN HAVE IT ALL   15

MYTH NO. 2:   GET A GOOD JOB AND
              YOU'LL BE SET FOR LIFE   20

MYTH NO. 3:   STOCKS ARE RISKY   29

MYTH NO. 4:   YOU CAN'T GO WRONG WITH IBM   48

MYTH NO. 5:   YOU CAN BEAT THE MARKET   54

MYTH NO. 6:   YOUR INVESTMENTS WILL
              MAKE 10 PERCENT A YEAR   63

MYTH NO. 7:   YOU CAN'T GO WRONG
              WITH MUTUAL FUNDS   70

MYTH NO. 8:   YOU CAN FIND THE NEXT
              MAGELLAN   85

MYTH NO. 9:   INDEX FUNDS ARE GUARANTEED
              MEDIOCRITY   95

MYTH NO. 10: NOTHING'S SAFER THAN
              MONEY IN THE BANK   102

MYTH NO. 11: IF YOU NEED INCOME, BUY BONDS   108

CONTENTS

MYTH NO. 12: HEDGE YOUR BETS WITH HARD ASSETS   120

MYTH NO. 13: YOU SHOULD OWN A BALANCED
PORTFOLIO   126

MYTH NO. 14: YOU NEED A BROKER   136

MYTH NO. 15: KEEP SIX MONTHS OF
EMERGENCY MONEY   151

MYTH NO. 16: DEBT IS DANGEROUS   157

MYTH NO. 17: BUY THE BIGGEST HOUSE POSSIBLE   166

MYTH NO. 18: YOU CAN'T BEAT THE
MORTGAGE TAX DEDUCTION   172

MYTH NO. 19: INVEST IN YOUR HOUSE   180

MYTH NO. 20: TRADE UP AS SOON AS YOU CAN   184

MYTH NO. 21: PROTECT AGAINST EVERY DISASTER   190

MYTH NO. 22: LIFE INSURANCE IS A GOOD
INVESTMENT   198

MYTH NO. 23: INVEST IN YOUR KID'S NAME   203

MYTH NO. 24: MAX OUT YOUR IRA EVERY YEAR   211

MYTH NO. 25: ONE DAY, KIDS, ALL OF THIS
WILL BE YOURS   218

CONCLUSION: THE NEW RULES FOR FINANCIAL
SUCCESS   226

INDEX   230

25 Myths You've Got to Avoid— If You Want to Manage Your Money Right

HOW YESTERDAY'S RULES BECAME TODAY'S MYTHS

Everybody needs somebody to blame. I'm blaming my parents. It's unfair, of course. They brought me up, they educated me, they taught me to put the fork on the left. But it's the late 1990s, the world isn't working the way they said it would and I need somebody to blame. Sorry, Ma.

It's not entirely her fault. After all, Dad also deserves some blame. But the real problem is, everything changed. Fixed pensions became unhinged. Cherished employees became temporary labor. Home prices plummeted. Inflation disappeared. Folks kept living longer. Wages stopped rising. And Harvard started charging $100,000 for four years.

All of which means the old financial rules don't work anymore. Remember what our parents told us? Buy the biggest house you can. Nothing's safer than money in the bank. Take out the largest mortgage possible. You can't go wrong with IBM. Everybody should own gold. Stocks are risky. You ought to buy antiques. Remember Uncle Joey? He made a killing in antiques.

Remember?

This sort of foolishness hasn't gone away. But the messengers have changed. You hear this nonsense at parties, on the commuter trains, in the company bathroom, around the water cooler and at the community pool. Your friends and colleagues, who vowed they would never be like their parents, now parrot them endlessly.

Listen at your peril, because this free advice is usually worth what you are paying for it. (That's the reason we're charging serious money for this book. Honest.) With jobs so tenuous and saving for retirement so critical, you can't afford to make big mistakes with your money. You can't afford to buy lackluster investments and pursue wrong-headed financial strategies. You can't afford to get sucked in by the old wacky rules of thumb. These myths may be comforting mantras from the childhood dinner table. But they are still myths.

How did these myths develop? Some of them feed our egos, like the idea that we can beat the market or find the next superstar mutual fund. Some of them grow out of wishful thinking, like the belief that we can get rich buying expensive antiques and fixing up our homes. Some of the myths reflect our fears, like the need for lots of insurance and lots of emergency money. And some myths are old truths that worked once but have since been rendered obsolete by changing circumstances.

The fact is, a lot of the stuff our parents told us is now dead wrong. They didn't just mess us up. They messed everything up. But they also got very, very lucky. That's why we should despise them. They came of age when it really was morning in America. Stocks went up. Gold went up. Real estate went up. Jobs were plentiful. Things were just sickeningly good. (Unless, of course, you were African-American. Or a woman. Or gay. But that's another story.)

Now things are just okay. The gilded age has become the bronze age. Our job is to make the best of it. That's where this book comes in. It won't make you rich overnight. In fact, it may not make you rich at all. But it should help you avoid today's big pitfalls—and make the right financial moves—so that you can cope with financial emergencies, buy the right house, put your kids through college and retire in comfort.

With this book, I want to make you rethink all of your financial strategies. No, I don't expect you to agree with every one of my contentions. But I hope you will at least come to understand some of the flaws that imperil today's most popular money strategies.

Best of all, this book should confirm all of your worst suspicions about your parents and your colleagues and your friends. Yup, you were right all along. They really have been talking a lot of nonsense.

MYTH NO. **1**

YOU CAN HAVE IT ALL

So many desires, so little cash.

A big house. A snazzy car. An Ivy League education for the kids. A comfortable retirement. A financial safety net that includes heaps of insurance and a big cushion of cash. It's the shopping list of the American dream and you want it all. Guess what? You can't have it.

Of course, our parents didn't have it all, either. In fact, they lived rather modestly. But they brought us up to believe that the bounty of the world—plus the matching his and hers towel set—could all be ours, just as long as we worked hard, brushed our teeth and made our beds every morning.

What's the reality? The reality is, you aren't likely to ever have it all, no matter how hard you work (and forget the stuff about brushing your teeth and making your bed). Which means you have to learn to be choosy. You have to learn to be skeptical. You have to weigh the advice you hear very, very carefully. It's your money. Treat it well.

Where We Go Wrong

You shouldn't follow any financial strategy just because it says so in this book, or you read about it in *The Wall Street Journal,* or you heard some "guru" spouting on TV. Ditto for the advice you get from your financial advisers. After all, these folks have an agenda. They may want to help you, but meanwhile they are also helping themselves—to your money. The fact is, if you hang around too much with insurance agents, you will probably end up with too much life insurance. If you spend your days with real-estate agents, you will wind up owning an absurdly big house. If you talk too often to your broker, you will end up with too much money in broker-sold mutual funds. (The truth is, any money in broker-sold mutual funds is too much money. But we'll get to that later.)

And whatever you do, don't do what your brother-in-law says. Surveys show that most folks get their financial advice from friends and family. It's okay to listen to your uncle rattle on about his favorite investments. But you shouldn't do anything without first thinking carefully about the advice and whether it really makes sense.

You—and nobody else—have to make your life's critical financial decisions, knowing that you can't afford to do it all. So what should you do with your money? We all tend to share four major investment goals. We want to buy a decent house, put our kids through college, retire in comfort and be prepared for financial emergencies. But it's tough to meet all of these goals. Think of the dollars involved:

■ If you earn $60,000 a year and you want an emergency fund big enough to cover six months of living expenses, you need to sock away around $18,000. Just got a new job paying $70,000 a year? You will no doubt crank up your standard of living— which means your emergency reserve also has to be bigger.

■ Homes cost an average of $125,000, so making a 20 percent down payment is going to set you back some $25,000, and that's not counting all the closing costs. If you put down less than

20 percent, you have to pony up for mortgage insurance, which is obscenely expensive.

■ If you want to send your kid to a top private college, you are staring at a $100,000 bill for a four-year degree. Planning to have a second kid? The total tab just became $200,000.

■ If you want a portfolio big enough to provide you with $60,000 a year in retirement income, you need to amass around $1 million. That's a million in today's dollars. Every upward tick in consumer prices means your retirement portfolio has to be that much bigger.

The New Rules

Feeling overwhelmed? Start by deciding what's important to you. Maybe you want to buy a smaller house, knowing it will make it easier to send your kids to a great college. Maybe you want to skimp on housing and encourage your children to go to the local state university, so you can retire early. Or maybe you are willing to delay retirement, so you can live more lavishly and send your kids to a ritzy private school. None of these choices are bad. What's bad is not making a choice. Instead of staggering from one enormous credit-card bill to the next monthly car payment, you ought to decide what you want to achieve with your money and have a plan for how you are going to get there.

All the planning in the world, however, isn't worth squat if you don't save. You may not be able to have it all. But if you don't save, you won't have anything. Folks always have ample—and seemingly rational—excuses for not saving. I'll start next year, they promise. The market is too high, they cry. First, I have to buy a new car, they say. I've still got plenty of time, they argue. But the grim reality is, many folks never become serious savers. They squander money and time on purchases they don't even remember. So make a commitment. Start saving and start now.

If it helps, draw up a list of goals and stick it on your refrigerator. Announce to your friends and family that you plan to pay off your mortgage in 10 years, or retire at 55, or save $5,000 before the end of the year. Maybe their expectations will be the incentive that makes you stick with your plan. Consider tracking your investment progress using a spiral notebook or a computer program, so you see and appreciate what you achieve. For the financially ill-disciplined, personal-finance software programs such as Microsoft Money, Managing Your Money and Quicken can be surprisingly helpful. If you find it difficult to save, look into setting up an automatic investment plan, in which money is deducted from your paycheck or bank account every month and plopped straight into a mutual fund.

Don't overlook the virtues of being cheap. No, you don't have to recreate the life of Ebenezer Scrooge. But any dollar you choose to spend is a dollar you can't save, so think long and hard before you crack open your wallet. Remember, those dollars were awfully hard to come by and they are awfully hard to replace. If you are losing a third of your paycheck to federal, state, Social Security and Medicare taxes, it means you have to earn $1.50 to replace every dollar you spend. And when you do spend money, spend it only on things you really want. Venture to the stores with a shopping list and buy only the items that are on that list. So what if shopping is the national pastime? Refuse to join the game. Don't buy anything just because that's what your parents bought, or that's what your friends are buying, or that's what the television advertisements say you ought to buy.

Finally, pursue strategies that will make one dollar do the job of two. One of the key personal-finance challenges of the 1990s is learning to balance the conflicting pressures of job insecurity and the need to save for retirement. Because of job insecurity, there's an inclination to stick every available penny in easily accessible, conservative investments. But at the same time, because of the need to save for retirement, you really ought to shoot for top-flight investment returns by shoveling every spare dollar into stocks, especially stocks in tax-sheltered retirement accounts. An unresolvable conflict? Fortunately not.

There are strategies that will let you behave like a long-term investor, while still leaving you with easy access to your cash. As I

> ## *You Never Call, You Never Write*
>
> If you want to cut down on the amount you spend, try reducing temptation by putting an end to junk mail, mail-order catalogs and phone solicitations. You can slash the number of calls you receive from telephone salesmen by writing to the Telephone Preference Service, Direct Marketing Association, P.O. Box 9014, Farmingdale, NY 11735-9014. Make sure you include your name, address and telephone number, including area code.
>
> Meanwhile, stop much of your junk mail and mail-order catalogs by writing to the Mail Preference Service, Direct Marketing Association, P.O. Box 9008, Farmingdale, NY 11735-9008. When writing, include the different spellings of your name that are used in direct-mail solicitations.

suggest later in this book, you might want to put some of your emergency money in stocks, so the money grows more quickly and can eventually become a cornerstone of your retirement portfolio. Consider paying off your mortgage so that not only will you own your house outright, but also you will free up money every month that can be put toward college tuition. Keep your debts low and your financial obligations small, so you need less of an emergency reserve. Put your stocks in a margin account and set up a home-equity line of credit, so you can borrow money quickly and cheaply if you get hit with a financial cash crunch.

Magic solutions? Far from it. Even if you employ these strategies, you won't have it all. But with them, you should have a lot more than you otherwise would.

GET A GOOD JOB AND YOU'LL BE SET FOR LIFE

There may be folks in America who still believe this myth. But you could probably fit them in a Japanese import.

Re-engineering, restructuring, reorganizing, right-sizing. The irritating buzzwords of the management crowd have become the justification for corporate cruelty in the 1990s. Are these job cuts necessary? Maybe. Pleasant? Hardly. Worthy of glorification? Not in my book. For whatever buzzword you adopt, it means a job today, gone tomorrow.

But that's old news. Everybody now knows that corporations feel little loyalty toward their employees, so we all need the financial wherewithal to survive a prolonged period of unemployment. But the demise of corporate paternalism doesn't stop with pink slips. With the death of good jobs has come the death of good pensions. Unlike mass layoffs, the disappearance of traditional company pensions doesn't get the big newspaper headlines. But for many, that's where the sting really lies.

Where We Go Wrong

It's one of the biggest changes to hit the American work force in recent years. The advent of 401(k) plans, 403(b) plans, Simplified Employee Pension (SEP) plans, Keoghs and similar retirement-savings vehicles has meant the burden of saving and investing for retirement has been largely shifted from employers to employees. Before, you could count on a traditional company pension. The company provided the money for the pension plan. The company oversaw the investment of this money. After you retired, the company cut you a check every month. All you had to do, in return, was show a healthy dose of loyalty, sticking with a single company for long enough to secure decent pension rights.

But this comforting world is fast disappearing. Traditional company pension plans are being dismantled. Instead, the future of America's retirees has been put in our hands—the employees— a bunch of rank amateurs who have shown little inclination to save and no aptitude to invest intelligently. At first glance, this would not appear to be an entirely sensible arrangement. The drunks have, it seems, been put in charge of the distillery.

This Little Piggy Bank Went to Market

Confused by the bewildering array of retirement-savings plans? You're not alone. The tax rules involved are hideously complicated and even the folks who administer these plans often don't know all the ins and outs.

Here's a quick look at the nine main types of plan:

■ Individual retirement accounts (IRAs) can be set up by anybody with earned income. Your contributions are tax-deductible, unless you are covered by your employer's retirement plan, in which case the deduction phases out for couples earning more than $50,000 a year and single individuals earning above $30,000. These thresholds, which apply to the 1998 tax year, will rise over the next few years, thanks to the 1997 tax bill. The maxi-

---

mum allowable contribution is $2,000 per wage earner or $4,000 for a couple with a nonworking spouse.

■ The 1997 tax bill introduced a new type of IRA known as the Roth IRA. With this new IRA, you don't get an initial tax deduction. Unlike with a regular IRA, however, you can withdraw your contributions and any investment earnings without paying income taxes. You can contribute the full $2,000 to a Roth IRA only if you are a couple with earnings of less than $150,000 or are single with an income below $95,000. Moreover, each year your total combined contribution to IRAs—whether it's to a tax-deductible IRA or a Roth IRA—can't top $2,000. What if you don't qualify for either account? You can still make nondeductible contributions to a regular IRA.

■ With a 401(k) plan, you can typically contribute 15 percent of your salary up to an annual ceiling, which is currently $9,500. Your investments may earn matching contributions from your employer. While the investments offered in 401(k) plans vary enormously, a plan will often include a money-market fund, a bond fund and a few stock funds. The plan may also include the company's own stock and a guaranteed investment contract (GIC). GICs behave like souped-up certificates of deposit, but involve somewhat more risk. When you leave your job, you usually have the option of leaving the money in your employer's plan, rolling the money into an IRA or transferring the money to your new employer's plan.

■ If you are covered by a profit-sharing plan, your employer makes the contributions, not you. As the employee, you still have to decide how the money is invested, and as with a 401(k) plan, you can take the money with you when you quit your job. If you want your account to grow even faster, you may be able to make additional voluntary contributions that aren't tax-deductible.

■ A 403(b) plan has rules similar to those for a 401(k) plan. What are the differences? These plans, which are often made available to teachers and employees of nonprofit organizations, may let you contribute up to 25 percent of your salary, but the annual maximum is still $9,500. Participants are restricted to two types of investments, mutual funds and annuities. You don't like your choices? Unlike participants in a 401(k) plan, 403(b) plan participants—even if they haven't left their job—may be able to shift their money into individual 403(b) custodial accounts at, say, a brokerage firm or a mutual-fund company.

■ State, county and municipal employees often have 457 plans. Like 401(k) plans, 457 plans include an array of investment options. Employees can currently contribute up to $7,500 a year. Unlike participants in other employer-sponsored retirement-savings plans, however, 457 plan participants can't roll over their money into an individual retirement account when they leave their job. Instead, the money is usually left in the plan, where it continues to grow tax-deferred.

■ Keogh plans are popular with small businesses and those who are self-employed. Depending on your income and the type of Keogh plan, you or your employer might be able to contribute as much as $30,000 a year. Those with income from moonlighting can make tax-deductible contributions to a Keogh, even if they are also covered by their regular employer's retirement-savings plan.

■ Like Keoghs, Simplified Employee Pension plans are popular with small businesses and the self-employed. SEPs allow you or your employer to contribute as much as 15 percent of your salary each year, up to an annual dollar ceiling, which is currently $30,000. These accounts are often called SEP-IRAs because they are essentially individual retirement accounts with much higher contribution limits. Why pick a SEP over a Keogh? SEPs are less hassle to set up and manage.

■ A Savings Incentive Match Plan for Employees (SIMPLE), a new retirement plan for small businesses, allows you to contribute up to $6,000 a year. With these plans, you get a matching contribution from your employer. The annual contribution ceiling rises periodically, along with inflation.

With 401(k), 403(b) and other employer-sponsored retirement-savings plans, the size of your retirement nest egg depends on how much you choose to save and how good your investment decisions are. Larger companies offer 401(k) plans. Smaller businesses and the self-employed favor SEPs and Keoghs. Meanwhile, 403(b) plans are often used by hospitals, nonprofit groups, colleges and school districts. With some plans, the employer will give you money every year to invest. But oftentimes, your employer's contribution depends on how much you invest. Your employer might, for instance, toss in 50 cents for every dollar you contribute. What if you don't put in your share? You will have no retirement nest egg. Period.

Yet far too many employees act as if traditional company pensions still exist. They think they will get bailed out by the lottery, or rescued by an inheritance from their parents, or they can save for retirement after the kids are through college and the mortgage is paid off. Indeed, many folks put off saving for retirement until the last 10 or 15 years before they quit the work force, which may turn out okay, just as long as their employer doesn't push them into an unwelcome early retirement.

This is all a tad troubling, especially given current talk about scaling back Social Security, which is now a key source of income for many retirees. The Social Security system clearly needs to be fixed before it becomes too costly. But I worry about what will happen if the system is cut back too radically. We could have an entire generation of retirees who never got traditional company pensions and failed to take advantage of retirement-savings plans, but did pay a lifetime of Social Security taxes, only to find the benefits they receive are below those that their contributions should justify. Do we really want a generation of retirees spending their golden years under the Golden Arches, flipping burgers and eating happy meals?

The New Rules

But as worrisome as all this is, 401(k) plans and their ilk provide the educated, committed investor with an enormous opportunity. These plans may be dangerous for those who don't understand what's at stake, but they are a godsend for those who fully participate. If you save diligently and make sound investment decisions, you could amass a huge nest egg that will carry you comfortably through retirement and even provide a healthy inheritance for your kids or a sizable bequest to your favorite charity. With a traditional company pension, all you get is a stream of income that dies with you and your spouse. But with the new employer-sponsored retirement-savings plans, you own the underlying assets that generate the stream of income. If you do a rotten job of accumulating and managing these assets, you will suffer mightily in retirement. But if you do save regularly and invest intelligently, you can amass surprising riches.

Fortunately, it's fairly easy to be a good saver and a successful investor. Indeed, if you are going to save any money at all, there's no better deal than your employer's 401(k) or 403(b) plan. How come? You could get what I call the investor's triple play:

■ First, your retirement-plan contributions should be tax-deductible, so they come out of pretax dollars. How much is this tax savings worth? To get a sense, take a look at your marginal federal tax rate. That's the rate at which every additional dollar you earn is taxed. Everybody gets to earn some money tax-free each year, thanks to tax deductions and exemptions. After that, incremental income is taxed first at 15 percent. Once you get above certain thresholds, additional dollars are taxed at 28 percent, then 31 percent, then 36 percent and finally 39.6 percent. Whatever your last few dollars are taxed at, that's your marginal tax rate.

Suppose your marginal federal tax rate is 28 percent. If that's the case, every dollar invested in a tax-deductible retirement account is saving you 28 cents in taxes, so the real cost of the dollar invested is only 72 cents. If your investments are also tax-deductible at the state level, then the cost is even less. Moreover, because many people have their monthly or weekly contributions deducted from their paycheck, each investment is surprisingly painless. The money never passes through your hands, so it seems like less of a sacrifice. And because the money is deducted automatically, you can't skip contributions and it's troublesome to cancel entirely. Result? Unlike your diet or your exercise regimen, a 401(k) plan—once started—is something you are likely to stick with.

When saving for your retirement, aim to stash away at least 10 percent of your pretax income every year, with as much money as possible going into your employer's plan. If you want to retire before age 65 or if you don't start saving for retirement until your 40s, look to sock away an amount equal to 15 percent or even 20 percent of your pretax salary. Put the maximum possible in your employer's plan. Once you have hit the limit on your company plan, turn to other accounts for additional savings. And don't forget that the sooner you start, the more you will amass. Thanks to the extra years of investment earnings, $100 saved today is worth far more than $100 saved just four or five years from now.

■ Second, your retirement-plan contributions may be matched partially or entirely by your employer, so that every dollar you put in is good for another 50 cents or dollar from your company. Add that to the tax savings, and you may find that your contributions are garnering an immediate bonus of close to 100 percent. Yet a huge number of employees fail to sign up for 401(k) plans, thus losing the chance to get free money from their employer and Uncle Sam. Not participating in a 401(k) plan is possibly the dumbest investment mistake you can make.

■ Finally, your money grows tax-deferred until it's withdrawn. There's no annual tax bill for the interest earned by your bonds or the capital gains generated by your stocks. Instead, every dollar earned stays in the account, so that the dollars earn additional dollars and your retirement account gets the full benefit of investment compounding. Compounding is the wondrous process by which money grows. If you have $1,000 that earns 8 percent a year, your account will grow by $80 to $1,080 at the end of the first year. What happens in the following year? If you again earn 8 percent, your account will grow by $86 to $1,166, with the higher dollar gain reflecting the fact that you started the year with more money. And so it continues, with your 8 percent annual gain bolstering the account to $1,260 after three years, $1,360 after four years, $1,469 after five years, $2,159 after 10 years, $4,661 after 20 years and $21,725 at the end of 40 years.

Your nest egg would fatten even faster if you regularly added to it. Say you started with $1,000 and then put in $1,000 every year thereafter. An 8 percent annual gain would give you $16,645

Don't Count on Quitting Early

Many folks say they want to quit the work force before age 60. Most won't manage it. In fact, they won't even come close. To amass enough to retire early, you really need to save at least 20 percent of your pre-tax salary every year for 25 years. That's a huge amount to sock away each year, and most people just aren't willing to make the necessary sacrifices.

Moreover, simply saving like crazy isn't enough. You may have to continue living fairly frugally even after you quit the work force. In addition, both before and during retirement, you will need to invest aggressively by keeping a hefty chunk of your portfolio in stocks.

Why does early retirement involve such extreme measures? Saving enough to retire is tough at the best of times. But the hurdle is especially high for early retirement wannabees. How so? First, you have less time to save. Second, your portfolio has less time to grow before you start tapping it for income. Finally, you will spend more time in retirement, so your savings have to last longer.

after 10 years, $50,423 after 20 years and $280,781 at the end of 40 years.

But this impressive progress would slow, halt or even reverse if you stopped contributing money or withdrew some. The biggest danger arises when you switch employers. Before the proliferation of 401(k) plans, changing jobs was often a losing proposition, because you ended up sacrificing your pension rights. But with the new retirement-savings plans, you can keep your nest egg alive and growing, just so long as you follow the rules.

If you change jobs and you have money in your company's retirement-savings plan, you may be able to leave it in your old employer's 401(k) plan, roll it over into your new employer's plan or roll it into an individual retirement account. But either deliberately or by accident, many folks end up cracking open their retirement nest egg when they change jobs, thus triggering a massive income-tax bill on the amount withdrawn, plus a 10 percent tax penalty for taking money out before age 59½. Deliberate withdrawals are self-inflicted wounds that are hard to heal and even harder to comprehend, because it is often impossible to fix the damage done to your future retirement lifestyle.

Accidental withdrawals are more understandable, though often equally damaging. Problems occur if you opt to take possession of your retirement funds, rather than rolling over your 401(k) money. At that point, your old employer sends you a check, but only for 80 percent of the account balance. The other 20 percent goes to the Internal Revenue Service. You can claim back that 20 percent on your next tax return, but only if you roll over your entire 401(k) balance into another retirement account within 60 days. That's not as easy as it sounds, because you don't have your entire account balance, but rather just 80 percent. Unless you can rustle up the other 20 percent, you are out of luck. The 20 percent you didn't roll over will get hit with a brutal combination of income taxes and the 10 percent tax penalty. If you are in the 28 percent tax bracket, for every dollar you fail to roll over, you will lose 38 cents—28 cents to income taxes and 10 cents for the penalty. You also, of course, lose the chance to let the money continue growing tax-deferred, which may turn out to be the biggest loss of all.

I am not saying you should never crack your nest egg. There may be circumstances in which it's justified, especially if you lose your job or get hit with a major medical emergency. Under certain circumstances, you may even be able to avoid the 10 percent tax penalty. But in general, if you are tempted to tap your retirement accounts, the advice is simple and succinct: Don't do it.

STOCKS ARE RISKY

We aren't scared of stocks. We're petrified.

This isn't entirely unjustified. There was, after all, the Great Crash, the gruesome bear market that saw the Dow Jones Industrial Average plunge 89 percent between 1929 and 1932. More recently, we had the 1973–74 market debacle, when the 30 Dow stocks were bludgeoned 45 percent over two years. And let's not forget the 1987 crash, with its 36 percent drop in two months, or the 1990 bear market, when the Dow stocks shed 21 percent. These percentage losses reflect changes in share prices. They don't take into account the dividends paid out by the companies involved, which would have partially cushioned each of these terrifying market drops. But even if you included dividends, the lesson would be the same: Bear markets are nasty, brutish and they aren't always short.

This sort of market turmoil rolls around with alarming frequency. Over the past seven decades, stocks have posted 20 calendar-year losses, according to Ibbotson Associates, a Chicago research firm. Often, it isn't pretty. The 500 larger companies in the Standard & Poor's 500-stock index have taken some nasty one-year hits, including double-digit losses of 24.9 percent in 1930, 43.3 percent in 1931, 35 percent in 1937, 11.6 percent in 1941, 10.8 percent in 1957, 10.1 percent in 1966, 14.7 percent in 1973 and 26.5 percent in 1974. These figures reflect the S&P 500's total return, which means they include both share-price changes and dividends.

Frightened? In truth, broad averages like the S&P 500 and the Dow Jones Industrial Average don't tell the whole story. Even when the indexes are rising smartly, individual stocks—especially small-company stocks—can suffer brutal losses. Wall Street is fond of ritual bloodlettings, slashing 20 percent or 30 percent off a company's stock price because of a weak earnings report or a slight sales slowdown.

It's enough to make grown men cry. Many do.

Where We Go Wrong

So are stocks risky? You bet. Stocks are undoubtedly risky, if you define risk as the chance of a large short-term loss. But if you are a long-term investor, there's a lot more to fret about than just market gyrations, and arguably short-term losses are the least of your worries. Investing involves all kinds of risks. There's the risk that a single company goes bankrupt or defaults on its interest payments, thus hurting owners of the company's stocks and bonds. There's the risk that you bail out of stocks, anticipating a decline in prices, only to see prices roar ahead. There's the risk that you panic when stock prices drop, dumping your holdings and thus locking in your losses.

But for long-term investors, all these risks pale beside the biggest risk of all—the risk that the value of your money will get whittled away by inflation and taxes, so that you can't meet your financial goals. When the market declines, we all wonder whether our money will still be there tomorrow. But that's a fleeting concern. Because of the twin threats of inflation and taxes, what we should really worry about is whether our money will be there many years from now, when we retire.

With consumer prices in the 1990s rising at annual rates of 3 percent and less, inflation might seem like a piffling concern. But even 3 percent inflation can be devastating. At that rate, the spending power of a dollar is cut in half in just over 23 years. Inflation and taxes present investors with a daunting challenge. If your investments don't earn enough to beat back this challenge, the purchasing power of your money will slowly shrivel. Sure, it's not as dramatic as a market crash. But the one-two punch of inflation and taxes can be far more devastating.

Viewed from that perspective, stocks aren't particularly risky. When you buy shares, you buy an ownership stake in American or foreign corporations. While some companies will slide into bankruptcy, most will thrive. As corporate profits rise, this drives stock prices higher and allows companies to pay ever-larger quarterly dividends. Rising wages and escalating raw-material costs could potentially crimp profits. But often, companies are able to pass along these rising costs to consumers. In fact, earnings typically rise faster than inflation—and so, too, do stock prices. Result? While accelerating inflation may spook the market and drive down share prices in the short term, over the long haul stock investors are protected against rising consumer prices.

By contrast, more conservative investments such as bonds and money-market funds offer only a feeble defense against inflation and taxes, making them a rotten choice for long-term investors. Indeed, if you are to have any hope of retiring in comfort or amassing at least a portion of the money needed to pay for your youngster's college education, you need the sort of returns that only the stock market can deliver. For better or worse, stocks—like relatives—are something you have to learn to live with.

After a while, you could even come to like the dear things. If you have the patience and the tenacity to hang on, few investments will make you as wealthy as stocks. If you invest in a broad collection of stocks—which is what you get with most stock-mutual funds—you should at least break even over five years. If you tough it out for a decade, you can be fairly confident of outpacing inflation, bonds, certificates of deposit and money-market funds. Over a lifetime of investing, your stocks will likely beat inflation by between six and seven percentage points a year. Presuming inflation runs at around 3 percent a year, that translates into an annual return of close to 10 percent. If you manage to earn seven percentage points a year more than inflation, the real, inflation-adjusted value of your money would double after 10 years, quadruple after 20 years and increase eightfold after 30 years.

Yet statistics like that are apparently scant comfort to investors. For many of us, the biggest pitfall isn't the vicissitudes of the market. Rather, the problem is our own emotional turmoil. We are, it seems, timid investors by nature. According to the experts in behavioral finance, we get more pain from losses than pleasure from gains, so there's a natural inclination to favor more conservative investments. Moreover, we tend to fixate on returns over a single year, which makes it tough to own stocks, which prove their worth over the long haul.

Sound bad? It gets worse. We often hang on to losing investments too long, waiting to break even, while selling winning investments too quickly, because the realized gain is so much more comforting than the paper profit. We also tend to dwell on those investments that do poorly, rather than considering their returns in the context of our overall portfolio's performance. At the same time, we assume that the high-flying securities owned by others will keep on flying high. The result is that we dump lackluster investments before they get a chance to prove their worth and pile into winning investments just before they fizzle.

Consistent? Not us. Behavioral-finance experts say that we're more likely to invest aggressively with windfall gains like lottery winnings and year-end bonuses, while sticking with conservative investments for the money we wring from our weekly paycheck. We might dabble in risky initial public stock offerings and dicey aggressive-growth mutual funds, but at the same time insist on owning only supersafe bonds issued by the U.S. Treasury. We are unjustifiably confident in our ability to pick successful investments and yet we are also worried about our lack of self-control. To compensate for our ill-disciplined ways, we like retirement accounts, with which there are penalties for early withdrawals, and automatic investment plans, in which money is pulled out of our bank account or paycheck every month and put directly into a mutual fund.

What should we make of all this? The picture sure isn't pretty and the conclusion is all too obvious. Yup, when it comes to investing, we're a bunch of irrational, inconsistent, neurotic wimps.

For some, the potential gains from stock-market investing can in no way compensate for the associated agony. These folks find the market's daily fluctuations simply too stressful. My advice: Stay away from stocks. There is no point in ruining your health for the sake of achieving riches. But if you can, you should overcome your aversion to short-term losses and learn to live with the market. It's not easy. You will make mistakes and you will get rattled by market declines. Everybody does. Indeed, in my experience, the pros are often more edgy than the amateurs. Maybe it's because they watch the markets too closely. Maybe it's because they fret not only about losing money, but also about losing their jobs. But whatever the reason, if even the professional stock jockeys find investing stressful, don't be surprised if you too have your queasy moments.

The New Rules

It's easy to convince yourself that stocks are the least risky choice. It's a lot tougher to act as if you really believe it. You may be able to accept intellectually that long-run inflation is a bigger danger than short-term market fluctuations. But somehow, this isn't quite so apparent when the world seems to be going to hell and your portfolio is going with it. What should you do? Unfortunately, if you invest in stocks, you can't avoid all the terror of the market. But here are five strategies that will help blunt the pain.

Play It Again and Again, Sam

A favorite strategy among investors is so-called dollar-cost averaging, which involves investing a fixed amount on a regular basis, usually every month. The idea is, when stocks are lower, your monthly investment will buy more shares. When prices are higher, your money buys less. Because stock prices rise over time, you should eventually own shares that are worth a lot more than the price you paid.

Most folks end up dollar-cost averaging without even knowing they are doing it. When they get paid every month or every week, they take some small part of their paycheck and sock it away in a stock-mutual fund. They end up investing on a regular basis, because that's how they get paid.

Though born of necessity, dollar-cost averaging has three pleasant side effects. First, it takes a lot of the emotion out of buying stocks, because your investing is effectively put on autopilot. Second, it eliminates the risk of putting all your money into stocks at a market peak. Third, it helps to make investors more tenacious. When stock prices rise, you have the pleasure of getting richer. When the market falls, you have the comfort of knowing that your next investment will buy shares at a lower price. Yet in recent years, dollar-cost averaging has come under attack. This assault is a bunch of academic nonsense and you should do your best to ignore it. But just in case somebody tries to convince you that you shouldn't use dollar-cost averaging, here's what the debate is all about.

Some academics, as well as assorted other experts, say that if you want the highest possible returns, you should throw everything into the market right away, rather than investing your money gradually. This is entirely correct, though totally irrelevant. Why are the eggheads correct? It's simple logic. Stocks rise over time. If you put your money into the market earlier rather than later, you are likely to get higher returns. One study, by Wright State University professors Richard E. Williams and Peter W. Bacon ("Lump Sum Beats Dollar-Cost Averaging," *Journal of Financial Planning,* April 1993), looked at over six decades of stock-market performance. The study found that you would have earned better returns 64.5 percent of the time if you had thrown your money into the market right away rather than investing it gradually over the next 12 months.

This sort of number crunching may keep folks busy, but the information itself is utterly useless, for two reasons. First, we can't throw all our wealth into the market right away, because we don't have the money yet. We are waiting for our next paycheck, and the paycheck after that, and the paycheck after that. Second, when we do have a large sum to invest, we don't invest the money gradually because we believe this will lead to the highest possible return. Rather, we invest gradually to reduce risk. We don't want to take the chance of throwing everything into the market and then immediately seeing the money devoured by a stock-market crash. Dollar-cost averaging may not lead to the highest possible return, but it's an excellent stock-market buying technique for ordinary investors. My advice: Ignore the eggheads. Slow and steady investing will win the race.

Spread Your Bets

If you want to reduce the risk of stock-market investing, you have to diversify. That means buying lots of stocks, some big "blue-chip" stocks, some little companies, some high-flying growth stocks, some dirt-cheap dull companies, some U.S. stocks, some foreign stocks. By diversifying, you reduce the chance that your portfolio will get badly hurt by one or two rotten stocks or one or two rotten market sectors.

The standard advice on Wall Street is that you need at least 12 to 20 companies to get decent diversification. But a recent paper, written by University of Nevada at Las Vegas professors Gerald D. Newbould and Percy S. Poon ("Portfolio Risk, Portfolio Performance, and the Individual Investor," *Journal of Investing,*

Hitting All the Bases

When it comes to investing in stock funds, it seems one is never enough. Most funds are quite specialized, investing in just a single part of the global stock market, so you may need as many as half a dozen funds if you want to tap all the major market sectors. As you build your stock portfolio, aim to have exposure to six areas.

LARGE-COMPANY GROWTH STOCKS

Often these companies, such as Coca-Cola, General Electric and Merck, appear pricey compared to other stocks. But there's a reason for that. These blue-chip stocks, as larger companies are often called, hold out the promise of rapid and reliable earnings and revenue growth. And earnings growth, over the long haul, is what drives the market.

If you look at the stock tables in many daily newspapers, you will see stocks quoted at a multiple of their per-share earnings. Sometimes, this price-earnings multiple is rich, with a company's stock valued at 18 or more times the firm's per-share earnings for the preceding 12 months. For instance, if the company earned $1.50 a share over the past year and its stock was at $30, its price-earnings ratio would be 20. At other times, when investors are less exuberant, the P/E ratio might be only 10 or 12.

But the earnings multiple that a company trades at is the stuff of short-term market sentiment. What counts over the long haul is earnings. If a company's per-share earnings triple, its stock may not rise in lockstep. But there's a good chance the shares will post a gain of similar magnitude.

When hunting for growth-stock funds, don't be misled by traditional fund categories such as "growth," "aggressive growth" and "growth and income." Funds are slotted into these categories depending on whether they emphasize dividend income or share-price appreciation when picking stocks. For instance, in most mutual-fund classification systems, a growth fund is a fund that buys stocks that are likely to provide most of their gain through share-price appreciation rather than dividend income. These growth funds don't necessarily buy growth stocks.

LARGE-COMPANY VALUE STOCKS

If you are looking for rapid earnings gains, value stocks aren't nearly as enticing as their growth-stock competitors. But they have a different virtue: They're cheap. Value stocks, such as Exxon, General Motors and Mobil, typically look like bargains based on market yardsticks such as price-to-earnings ratio, dividend yield and share-price-to-book value.

Dividend yield is the value of the dividend paid out by a company over the past 12 months, divided by the firm's share price. A $40 stock that pays 25 cents a quarter, or one dollar a year, would have a dividend yield of 2.5 percent. Meanwhile, book value is the difference between a company's assets and its liabilities, expressed on a per-share basis. Book value represents the amount of money that shareholders have sunk into a company through startup capital, subsequent share offerings and retained earnings.

Because of their lackluster earnings growth, value stocks might seem like a poor bet. But historically, they have performed well. How come? Just as investors are often overly optimistic about the earnings prospects of growth companies, so they tend to be too downbeat about the outlook for value stocks. Result? Value companies are frequently priced too cheaply and end up performing well when the companies surprise the market by posting good business results.

SMALL-COMPANY GROWTH STOCKS

How small is small? It's a subject of some debate. I would classify a company as small if its stock-market value is less than $2 billion. But some set the hurdle far lower, at $200 million or less. Academic research, notably the work by Rolf W. Banz ("The Relationship Between Return and Market Value of Common Stocks," *Journal of Financial Economics* vol. 9, 1981), suggests that the very smallest stocks—both growth and value—tend to outperform large-company stocks.

Like blue-chip growth stocks, small-company growth stocks promise rapid revenue and earnings growth, and the stocks are priced accordingly. Typically, however, the price paid—and the growth promised—is even greater with smaller companies. When the growth is delivered as expected, these stocks can soar. But if growth falters, look out below.

SMALL-COMPANY VALUE STOCKS

Just as investors are often too downbeat about the prospects for large-company value stocks, they also tend to be excessively pessimistic about the outlook for small-company value stocks. Betting on these smaller stocks, however, is even more dicey, in part because the companies often have only one line of business and thus are more vulnerable to new competition and new market trends.

But this extra risk seems to bring with it extra reward. Indeed, academic research by Eugene F. Fama and Kenneth R. French ("The Cross-Section of Expected Stock Returns," *Journal of Finance,* June 1992) has suggested that small-company value stocks are the best-performing part of the market over the long haul. These stocks typically have slimmer dividend yields than blue-chip value companies, though they are sometimes cheaper based on other market yardsticks.

DEVELOPED FOREIGN MARKETS

The United States is the world's largest stock market, as measured by the value put on American corporations. But some 57 percent of the world stock market is now located outside the United States, up from just 34 percent in 1970. That doesn't mean, however, that you should put 57 percent of your money abroad. Rather, I would argue that you might aim to have up to 30 percent of your stock-market money in foreign stocks, with much of this money in developed markets such as France, Germany, Japan and the United Kingdom.

When you invest in these developed foreign markets, you should earn long-run returns roughly comparable to those you could enjoy by buying U.S. stocks. So why bother investing abroad? Foreign stocks sometimes sparkle when U.S. shares are suffering, so you can smooth out the bumps in your overall portfolio's performance by including some overseas investments.

Currency swings generate much of this diversification advantage. When the dollar falls, that boosts the value of foreign stocks for U.S. investors. But if the dollar climbs, U.S. holders of foreign stocks lose money. That prompts some to argue that you should buy foreign-stock funds that "hedge" their foreign-currency exposure and thereby eliminate these currency swings. But in truth, you want the currency swings, because they may work to bolster your foreign-stock holdings at a time when U.S. stocks are suffering.

EMERGING MARKETS

Emerging markets are often seen as the most treacherous part of the global stock market. But just as the addition of developed foreign markets can reduce the risk level of a U.S. stock portfolio, so you get some added diversification by including a small investment in emerging markets. The real reason you want to include such emerging markets as South Korea, Malaysia and Mexico, however, is to boost returns. Many emerging-market economies are growing three times as fast as the U.S. economy, and that means there's the chance for companies to chalk up extraordinarily rapid earnings growth and corresponding share-price increases.

How should you use the above six categories? Many stock funds specialize in one of these six sectors, so you could build a well-diversified portfolio by buying one fund from each category. But not every fund can be so neatly classified. Some funds, for instance, invest in all six sectors. Others invest in only a portion of one sector. What should you do? Start by deciding how many stock funds you want to own and work from there. Whether you choose to buy three or six or a dozen stock funds, make sure your collection of funds gives you exposure to all six sectors.

Summer 1996), argues that this number is far too low. The study suggests that, if you are going to eliminate most of the risk that your portfolio will get severely punished by laggard stocks, you really need to own at least 60 companies in your blue-chip stock portfolio and 100 companies in your small-stock portfolio.

How can you possibly get exposure to that many stocks? Mutual funds are your best bet. With funds, you can acquire a slew of different stocks, without all the trading costs and paper-work hassles involved in buying individual securities. Indeed, I believe funds should be the core of every investor's stock portfolio, accounting for between 70 percent and 100 percent of the money invested. If you fancy yourself as a stock picker, you might put up to 30 percent of your stock portfolio into individual stocks. But with my own portfolio, I am reluctant to put any money into individual securities.

With an individual stock, you can get hit hard if earnings falter, or the chief executive turns out to be a crook, or the company's product proves defective, or new competitors muscle into the field. Even when a stock seems like a slam-dunk, surefire winner, you can still be blindsided. Because of this risk, I would make sure that no individual stock accounts for more than 5 percent of your total stock-market portfolio. This rule of thumb applies even if it's your employer's stock. In fact, you should be especially leery of holding your own company's stock. Suppose your employer falls on hard times. What happens? You could end up both unemployed and holding a fistful of worthless shares.

With mutual funds, which own a bevy of stocks, this individual-company risk is pretty much eliminated. Sure, a few of the fund's holdings will fall out of bed each year. But this isn't going to put a big dent in the fund's share price. Don't, however, presume that funds are a panacea. They aren't. Many are highly specialized. Indeed, to get decent diversification, you may have to buy half a dozen or more funds, each representing a different market sector.

By diversifying across a fistful of funds, you don't just eliminate the risk of owning a single rotten stock. You also reduce the risk that your portfolio will get badly hurt because a single sector of the market goes out of favor for an extended period. If large U.S. stocks fall from grace, the blow may be cushioned by strong performance from smaller stocks or foreign stocks. In a vicious bear market, all sectors will tend to get hammered, but they won't all decline equally. By diversifying, you ensure that your portfolio won't get hit as hard as the hardest-hit sector.

Cushion the Blows

Spreading your money among a variety of stocks and over a host of market sectors will mellow your portfolio. But life could still be mighty unpleasant. If the stock market goes into a tailspin, so will your stocks and funds. What if you want to tame your portfolio even further? Look to other investments. You have four main choices. But some of them, I believe, make a lot more sense than others.

■ *Cash.* What's that? It's stuff like Treasury bills, certificates of deposit, bank money-market accounts, savings accounts and money-market mutual funds, where there's little or no chance that you will lose money. But this peace of mind comes with a steep price tag: Cash investments generate lousy long-run returns. Nonetheless, cash can be a great way to diversify a stock portfolio. How come? When stocks take a tumble, you can be sure that your cash won't.

■ *Bonds.* If you buy a bond and hold it to maturity, you get a fair amount of certainty. You know how much interest you will receive each year and you know how much you will get back when the bond matures. But are bonds a good way to diversify a stock portfolio? Not always.

The problem is, some market menaces—such as rising interest rates and the specter of inflation—will pummel both bonds and stocks. Bond prices and interest rates move in opposite directions, so that when interest rates rise, bond prices dive. Bonds, however, may not fall quite as hard as stocks, so adding them to the mix could slow your portfolio's descent. What if stocks plunge for other reasons, such as a political crisis or a slowdown in economic growth? In these situations, bonds may prove their worth, rising or treading water even as stocks fall.

■ *Hard Assets.* Financial assets such as stocks and bonds can tumble for all sorts of reasons. But accelerating inflation is possibly the biggest threat. What to do? You could add hard assets to your portfolio. Collectibles, gold, real estate and other hard assets are champions at maintaining their value relative to inflation, so investors flock to these assets at times of rapidly rising consumer prices. Indeed, hard assets were stellar performers in the inflationary 1970s. But while hard assets may keep up with inflation over the long haul, that's about as good as it gets. You won't make much money, over and above the inflation rate, so hard assets turn out to be a poor long-run investment.

■ *Contrarian Strategies.* If you are concerned that the market will tumble, you can pursue various contrarian strategies or buy a mutual fund that will pursue these strategies for you. You might, for instance, "sell short" some seemingly overpriced stocks by borrowing the stocks from a brokerage firm and then selling them, in a bet that the shares will fall. Alternatively, you could short the entire market, using options and futures. If the market tumbles, these investments will make you money, thus providing gains to offset the losses in your regular stock-market investments. The trouble is, contrarian strategies face an uphill battle. Stocks rise over time. If you bet that the market or individual stocks will fall, the odds suggest you will be wrong far more often than you are right—and your portfolio's long-run performance will suffer accordingly.

Keep Your Balance

Rebalancing is possibly the most overlooked risk-reduction strategy. What is rebalancing? It involves setting targets for what percentage of your money should be in particular investments and then, every year or so, readjusting your portfolio to bring it back into line with these targets.

You can rebalance both within your stock portfolio and across all investments. You might, for instance, have an investment mix of 60 percent stocks, 30 percent bonds and 10 percent cash. Because of strong stock-market returns, the stock portion might balloon to take up, say, 66 percent of your portfolio, while bonds dip to 26 percent and cash to 8 percent. To bring your portfolio back into line, you would cut back the stocks and add to your bond and cash holdings.

This is a fairly painless process if you do it in a retirement account, such as a 401(k) plan, a Keogh or an individual retirement account, because you don't have to worry about messy tax accounting when you sell securities. But if you are dealing with a taxable account or if you own investments where there are commissions charged when you buy and sell, rebalancing can be both costly and aggravating. What to do? If you add to your account regularly, consider using these dollars to bring your portfolio back into balance. Simply direct the new dollars to those investments that have become underweighted. You could also keep your portfolio in balance by taking the dividends, interest and mutual-fund distributions kicked off by your portfolio and using them to bolster those sectors that are lagging.

Rebalancing among stocks, bonds and cash controls your portfolio's risk level. If you don't rebalance, your stocks—as the best-performing investment—will come to take up an ever-greater portion of your portfolio, so that it becomes increasingly risky and could be hit hard by a market collapse. But while rebalancing controls risk, it doesn't usually help returns. After all, if your aim was the highest possible return, you would never cut back stocks and thus trim your portfolio's growth potential.

Rebalancing within a stock portfolio, however, has the potential to both reduce risk and increase returns. Suppose you rebalance a mix that includes 50 percent blue-chip stocks, 20 percent smaller companies and 30 percent foreign stocks. By rebalancing, you stop your portfolio from becoming overweighted in any one area, thus reducing the risk of a big hit if the overweighted sector suffers a reversal of fortune. What about boosting returns? Because stock-market sectors tend to cycle into and out of favor, there's the potential to boost returns if you take money away from areas that have recently done well—and could be due for a correction—and add it to those that have lagged and could be ripe for a rebound. But I wouldn't bank too heavily on this performance gain. Rebalancing is primarily about controlling risk. Any boost to returns should be considered a bonus.

Time Heals All Wounds

Dollar-cost averaging, diversifying and rebalancing can reduce the risk of stock-market investing. But there's only one thing that really heals stock-market wounds, and that's time.

If you have five or 10 years to invest, you should make decent money with stocks. But not always. In the five calendar years ending in December 1932, for instance, stocks lost almost half their value, as measured by the total return of the Standard & Poor's 500-stock index. There have even been a couple of 10-year stretches when stocks have fallen. According to Ibbotson Associates, the S&P 500 stocks fell modestly in the 10 years ending in December 1938 and the 10 years through December 1939.

Recent history has been kinder. Since the Second World War, there have been no 10-calendar-year periods when the S&P 500 has lost money and only two five-year stretches when these stocks have suffered a loss. During those five-year stretches, you could have muted the pain by diversifying broadly, investing regularly and including other investments, such as cash and bonds, in your portfolio. But no matter what you did, those five-year

Grand and Not-So-Grand Results

The charts that follow show how you would have fared if you had invested $1,000 in the Standard & Poor's 500-stock index, intermediate-term government bonds and Treasury bills. The numbers for worst performance reflect the most dismal calendar-year stretches during the 71 years since year-end 1925, while the amounts shown for average performance are based on average annual returns over this period. The charts show the value of your $1,000 at the end of the indicated period. The figures include not only gains or losses in security prices, but also the dividends and interest paid by the securities. The numbers, however, don't reflect inflation, which ran at 3.1 percent a year over the 71-year period.

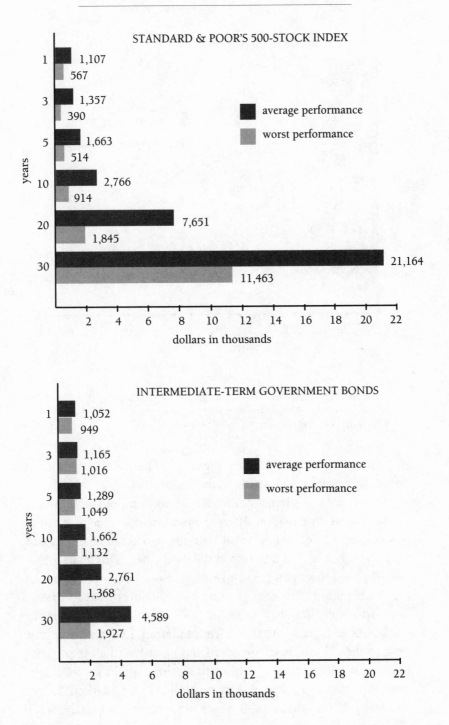

STANDARD & POOR'S 500-STOCK INDEX

■ average performance
■ worst performance

years

1 1,107
   567

3 1,357
   390

5 1,663
   514

10 2,766
   914

20 7,651
   1,845

30 21,164
   11,463

dollars in thousands

INTERMEDIATE-TERM GOVERNMENT BONDS

■ average performance
■ worst performance

years

1 1,052
   949

3 1,165
   1,016

5 1,289
   1,049

10 1,662
   1,132

20 2,761
   1,368

30 4,589
   1,927

dollars in thousands

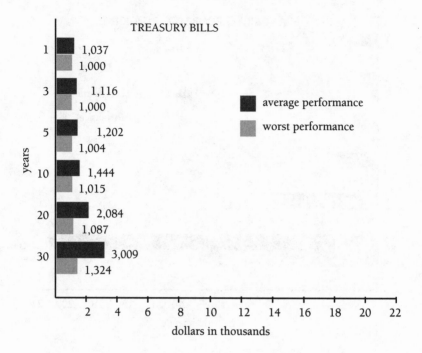

TREASURY BILLS

stretches wouldn't have been pleasant. There will, without a doubt, be similar rough spells in the future.

How can you prepare yourself? Try to think of stocks not as a one-year or five-year or 10-year investment, but as a lifetime preoccupation. Folks used to hit retirement, bail out of stocks and load up on bonds. But that was in the days when retirement might last 10 years. Now, you could live 25 years or longer after you retire. That's more than enough time for inflation to wreak havoc. But, fortunately, it's also plenty of time to make good money in stocks. Indeed, given the threat from inflation, I would argue that retirees should seriously consider keeping at least half their portfolios in stocks. People who are still working might keep 80 percent, 90 percent or more of their portfolios in the market. Risky? Not really. If you are 30 or 40 years old, you may own stocks for

50 or 60 years. You may even leave those stocks to your grand-children, who will own them for another 50 or 60 years. You may never sell some of your stocks. So who cares if the market hap-pens to tumble 10 percent or 20 percent tomorrow? It's not as though you need to sell your stocks any time soon.

YOU CAN'T GO WRONG
WITH IBM

With my mother-in-law, it's like a broken record. If only she could find the next Netscape. Or the next Boston Chicken. Or the next Home Depot. Sally likes the idea of initial public offerings, small hot mutual funds, small-company stocks. She doesn't just want to keep up with the market averages. She wants to win. Big time.

It's the lottery ticket mentality. All you need to do is throw one more quarter into the slot machine. You really can get rich overnight. Publishers Clearing House and its "prize patrol" really will appear on your doorstep with a fat check and a television camera. Lightning really does strike.

With investors like Sally, the tune is always changing. When they aren't dreaming of striking gold, they are waxing philosophical about the stock market's stalwart companies. They used to say, "You can't go wrong with IBM." But then IBM sat on the sidelines during the great bull market of the 1980s. So now folks say, "You can't go wrong with Microsoft."

Could you go wrong with Microsoft? The business world is ruthlessly competitive. Companies may briefly enjoy superior earnings growth and superior profit margins and that catches the attention of investors, who are a little too quick to believe that this advantage will persist. But most of the time, the superior returns attract fresh competition and competition quickly nixes the exceptional profitability that was previously enjoyed.

Maybe Microsoft will vanquish its competitors. Maybe you really can't go wrong with Microsoft. Maybe it will be the exception that proves the rule, the stock that keeps rising and rising and keeps the fantasy alive, while the many pretenders fall by the wayside.

On the subject of whether Microsoft can defy stock-market gravity, I have no opinion. But one thing is crystal clear to me. As an investor, it's not terribly important whether you own Microsoft or not. And if you do own the software giant, it's not terribly important whether Microsoft stumbles badly or continues its heady stock-market run.

Where We Go Wrong

Let me explain. The biggest driver of your portfolio's performance isn't whether you own 100 shares of Microsoft, or bought a top-notch bond fund, or guessed right on the direction of interest rates. You don't believe me? Consider:

■ It's the family New Year's party and Sue is feeling pretty good, and not simply because she's had a couple of drinks. Over the previous year, her bond fund had gained 7 percent, beating the 6.5 percent average for all bond funds, and her money-market fund had yielded 5 percent, more than the 4.5 percent average gain for all money funds. Sue had picked some winning funds and she couldn't be happier. With half her money in bonds and half in money funds, she clocked a one-year gain of 6 percent. Luckily, she isn't the designated driver.

■ Frank is the designated driver, but that's not the reason he's grumpy. Unlike Sue's, Frank's bond fund only matched the bond-fund average and his money-market fund merely kept up with the money-fund average. Moreover, his stocks also matched the market average, gaining 10 percent. Frank was clearly a dud at picking investments. With a third of his portfolio in stocks, a third in bonds and a third in cash, his gain for the year was 7 percent.

■ Joe is exuberant. He had half his portfolio spread equally among 20 stocks, and all but one of them gained 10 percent, matching the market average. But the final stock was a huge winner, soaring 50 percent. Like Sue, Joe also had the rest of his portfolio in one of the better money-market funds, which gained 5 percent. Result? Joe's portfolio was up 8.5 percent. Later, he will be wearing the lampshade.

■ Mary is even more gloomy than Frank. She prides herself on being a savvy investor and yet every one of her stocks failed to keep up with the market, gaining just 9.5 percent on average. But that 9.5 percent was also Mary's portfolio's return, because she was 100 percent in stocks.

Mary, of course, retires rich and happy. Joe and Frank do okay. Sue, meanwhile, pinches pennies until her final days, wondering all the time where she went wrong.

What's the lesson? Investors spend way too much time focusing on the wrong decisions. They diligently hunt for superstar mutual funds and super stocks, when they should be worrying about whether they have the right mix of investments. The most critical factor in a portfolio's performance isn't whether you own a top-flight bond fund, or 100 shares of Microsoft, or a chart-topping stock fund.

Instead, the key factor is your so-called asset allocation, how you divvy up your money among stocks, bonds, cash and other investments. Indeed, a study by Gary P. Brinson, L. Randolph Hood and Gilbert L. Beebower ("Determinants of Portfolio Performance," *Financial Analysts Journal,* July–August 1986) suggested that this basic mix explains 93.6 percent of the variability in portfolio returns. By comparison, everything else—picking the right stocks, guessing the direction of interest rates, hunting for the highest-yielding money-market fund—is inconsequential.

How can this be? Think about it. The reality is, most folks

don't own just one or two stocks. They own a portfolio of stocks. Your stock portfolio may beat or—more likely—lag behind the market. But however your stocks perform, their results aren't going to be radically different from the broad stock-market averages. Ditto for your holdings of bonds and cash. These, too, aren't likely to earn returns that are radically different from the average performance for all bonds and all cash investments.

Result? If you have half your money in stocks and the rest split between bonds and cash, you aren't likely to do as well as somebody who is wholly invested in stocks, no matter how good you are at picking investments. It's highly improbable that you will get stock-market returns by investing in bonds or cash. Fortunately, it's also highly unlikely that you will get bondlike or cashlike returns from owning a diversified portfolio of stocks.

All this would change, of course, if you weren't diversified. Some experts even advocate concentrating your money in a handful of stocks, so that you have a shot at earning high returns. Sound attractive? Believe me, it isn't. Yeah, you could roll the dice and pile everything on Microsoft, hoping it heads to the moon. But what if Microsoft goes the way of other stocks that were once favorites of investors? Over the past decade, we have seen the collapse of such once-celebrated growth stocks as Apple Computer, Discovery Zone, L.A. Gear and U.S. Surgical. These companies seemed like a one-way ticket to wealth, but their shareholders ended up as Wall Street road kill.

If you only own a handful of companies, you could trounce the market average—or get trounced. As you add stocks to your portfolio, you lower the odds of handily outpacing the market averages, but you also reduce the risk that your portfolio will get walloped by one or two rotten stocks. My view? The more stocks, the merrier. Stock-market investing is a nerve-wracking, nail-biting, stomach-churning endeavor. But for all the angst, the rewards have been impressive, just as long as you get something close to stock-market-average returns. If you diversify, that's the sort of returns you ought to get. What if you don't diversify? Let's just hope you are very lucky or very smart.

The New Rules

The bottom line? For most investors, it's not the performance of each individual investment that counts. Rather, what really matters is how these investors divide their money among the major financial assets. Microsoft may turn out to be a good investment. But you're still going to end up with lousy returns if you have 90 percent of your portfolio sitting in certificates of deposit. In other words, the more you have in stocks, the higher your portfolio's long-run performance. The more you have in bonds and cash, the lower your returns. This is the true secret of your portfolio's long-run success.

So what should determine your asset allocation? A lot of folks are told to act their age, putting more in stocks when they are young and less as they grow older. Indeed, a popular rule of thumb suggests that you subtract your age from 100. Whatever number you get, that's the percentage of your portfolio that you should put in stocks, with the rest of your money then shoveled into bonds and money-market funds. Thus, a 35-year-old would put 65 percent of his portfolio into stocks, while a 60-year-old ends up with 40 percent in stocks.

This isn't a bad rule of thumb. But I wouldn't use it. Partly that's because the portfolios generated tend to have too little in stocks for my taste. More important, the rule presumes that age is the most critical factor in determining your asset allocation. It just isn't so.

Instead, I would put a lot of emphasis on the time horizon. If you're a 65-year-old investing money for your 15-year-old grand-daughter's college education, you should be far more conservative with her college fund than you are with your own retirement money. After all, your granddaughter is going to college in just three years. Meanwhile, as a 65-year-old, you could well live another 25 years. With these two particular pools of money, your investment time horizon is a lot longer than your granddaughter's. So don't get hung up on age and instead pay attention to how soon you will need the funds. If you have money that you plan to spend in the next few years, you would be foolish to have that money invested in the stock market. But if you won't touch those dollars for 10 years or longer, you would be a fool not to own stocks.

While the time horizon is critical, risk tolerance is equally important. An investor's tolerance for risk is tough to nail down. We tend to be conservative. Which investors are more comfortable taking risk? It's not clear. Folks who seem like risk takers—they enjoy bungee jumping or parachuting—often have no stomach for stock-market gyrations. It seems our ability to keep our heads during market turmoil has nothing to do with our willingness to jump out of airplanes.

Moreover, our tolerance for risk changes over time. It's easy to be brave when stocks are rising, but it's a lot tougher when prices are tumbling. So how do you find out your risk tolerance? It's something you have to learn over time. If you have been investing for a while, look back at your own investment history, particularly how you reacted to falling markets and what prompted you to sell investments. This may be your best guide to how much risk you can really tolerate.

I believe investors should be heavily invested in the stock market. But you shouldn't do this if you are uncomfortable owning stocks. Not only will you be miserable, but you could also end up committing one of the cardinal sins of investing. What's that? If the markets plunge, you might panic and dump your stocks at the bottom of the market, thus locking in your losses and losing money you will never recoup. Even my mother-in-law knows you shouldn't do that.

YOU CAN BEAT THE MARKET

It's the big lie that, repeated often enough, is eventually accepted as truth.

You can beat the market. Trounce the averages. Outpace the index. Beat the Street. An entire industry stokes this fantasy. Newsletters promise to get you into stocks at market troughs and out at market peaks. Stock funds boast of their superior returns. Brokers offer tantalizing stock picks. Newspapers and personal-finance magazines tout hot investments. How could any red-blooded American deny the allure?

Not only are legions of investors convinced that it's possible to beat the market, many—I suspect—really believe that they themselves accomplish this feat. This conviction seeps into our language. We talk about how much we made in the market or how much we earned. Investors, of course, don't make money. Companies make money, which gets reflected in rising stock prices. Shareholders just go along for the ride. Yet we take credit for these gains, even as we disassociate ourselves from losses. When a stock falls apart, we blame the company's incompetent management. When a stock fund lags, it's the stupid fund manager's fault. When the market falls apart, we carp about those clowns in Washington.

Indeed, if you spend only a few minutes talking to most investors, all you will hear is a rundown of their greatest investment triumphs. It's like talking to folks about their driving. Some 90 percent will claim they are better than average. But if you want the real story, you will have to linger a little longer, because it's only then that folks start discussing all their investments that crashed and burned.

Beat the market? The idea is ludicrous. Very few investors manage to beat the market. But in an astonishing triumph of hope over experience, millions of investors keep trying.

Where We Go Wrong

Every investor, it seems, has his or her own peculiar strategy for outpacing the averages. But if you ignore all the nuances, you find these strategies typically fall into one of three broad categories: market timing, sector rotation and stock selection. Investors pursue these strategies either directly or through mutual funds. Each of the three strategies has its own unique flaws. But all of them share a common failing.

Market Timing

If you look at a chart of the Dow Jones Industrial Average or the Standard & Poor's 500-stock index, the key to investment success leaps off the page. All you have to do is get into stocks before the big rallies and bail out before the big dips. Simple, right? It seems not.

Successful market timers are rare indeed and, after you have invested for a while, it's easy to understand why. How many times have you seen the market tumble sharply over one or two days, prompting scary newspaper headlines, handwringing by friends and declarations of doom from market pundits? You, of course, become absolutely convinced that the end of the world will arrive before the weekend. Should you sell? Should you hang on? While you fret, the market bounces back, the crisis passes and you forget all about selling, until the next crisis.

Or maybe you are sitting on the sidelines, your money languishing in a savings account while you wait for your chance to buy stocks at fire-sale prices. The market is tumbling, but you think it will tumble further, so you wait. While you are still sitting on your hands, the market rallies spectacularly, the great buying opportunity passes and you kick yourself. The stock market often posts explosive gains in a matter of weeks or even days, so it's all too easy to miss a major market move. Indeed, a study commissioned by New York's Towneley Capital Management and conducted by University of Michigan professor H. Nejat Seyhun found that one dollar invested in the stock market from 1963 to 1993 grew to $24.30. But if you had missed the best 90 days, that dollar would have grown to just $2.10.

Like you, market timers must confront agonizing choices. Is this the beginning of a big drop or is it merely a blip along the way? Have stocks hit bottom or will they drop even more? You might think that earlier declines would offer some useful lessons. But when it comes to the market, past is rarely prologue. The market may be ridiculously overpriced by almost any historical measure and yet stocks will keep rising. Or stocks can seem dirt cheap compared to all standard market yardsticks, but prices still fall further. Because it's so tough to pick market peaks and troughs, many timers don't rely on intuition and fundamental analysis. Instead, they use mechanistic systems, bailing out of stocks when the market begins to trend down and jumping back in as stocks start to rise. But what seems like a market trend may turn out to be a temporary twitch, leaving timers whiplashed as they make a rash of unnecessary buys and sells. The result is missed opportunities, hefty trading costs, headaches at tax time and lackluster returns.

Many timers, in fact, concede that their chief aim isn't to boost returns, but to reduce risk. This is refreshingly honest. But it also shows why timing is so wrong-headed. For long-term investors, the biggest risk isn't short-term market declines. Rather, it is losing ground to inflation and taxes. If you want to combat that risk, you shouldn't jump into and out of stocks. Instead, you should buy stocks—and stick with them.

Sector Rotation

Sector rotation is like market timing, only it's more respectable. Instead of dashing between stocks and cash, depending on where you think the market is headed, you stick with stocks and switch among market sectors. Think small stocks are the place to be? You load up on these stocks, while lightening up on foreign stocks and blue-chip companies. Think growth stocks will sparkle? Boost your investment among these companies, while selling slower-growing value stocks.

The proliferation of mutual funds has made sector rotation—sometimes called style rotation—especially easy. Stock funds, after all, are just baskets of stocks. As funds have become more specialized, with some focusing on single-industry sectors or single regions of the global stock market, they have become the favored vehicle of folks who like to flit between market sectors, dumping one and diving into another.

But it's not clear that all this activity accomplishes very much. True, by sticking with stocks, you avoid the risk of being out of the market when stock prices surge. But you can still get caught with too much money in a lackluster market sector, while other sectors roar ahead. Like market timers, sector rotators often end up in the wrong place at the wrong time, meanwhile incurring hefty trading costs and creating tremendous tax hassles. Tempted to rotate? Just say no.

Stock Selection

While Wall Street has come to look dimly on sector rotation and market timing, the virtues of individual stock selection are still trumpeted. Sure, it's tough to be right on the big market bets, say the professional stock jockeys. But if you roll up your sleeves and really study your stocks, you can find gems that lazier investors have overlooked.

The problem is, in the investment business, there are a lot of folks with rolled-up sleeves, which means there aren't a lot of undiscovered gems. Wall Street is full of bright analysts and bright portfolio managers with business degrees and fancy computers and unsurpassed work habits, all rooting around for winning stocks. When you buy or sell a stock, you might well be buying from or selling to one of these folks. Do you really know more than they do?

The New Rules

Each of the three favored strategies has its own drawbacks. But surely some investors—whether through luck or through skill—will come out ahead by switching into the right sectors, or timing the market, or picking winning stocks? Some do indeed manage this, but far fewer than you might imagine. Consider for a moment the odds involved. Taken together, stock-market investors can't beat the market, because collectively we are the market. As a matter of logic, it couldn't be any other way. But even this understates the odds that investors face, because it ignores investment costs. Before investment costs, investors may collectively match the market averages. But once investment costs are figured in, most folks will trail the market. Indeed, taken together, investors will trail the market by an amount equal to the investment costs they incur.

But don't just accept my logic. Look at the statistics. The most public failures are stock mutual funds. Funds get their returns published in the newspaper every day and their performance is frequently audited, so there's no chance to monkey with the results. How have funds fared? They lag behind the market averages with alarming regularity, typically by about two percentage points a year. Even the published performance numbers, however, don't tell the whole story. While the results you see in the newspaper reflect annual mutual-fund expenses, they don't take into account mutual-fund sales commissions and taxes. After these are figured in, investors lag the market by far more than two percentage points a year.

Could you do better than most stock-fund investors? I think so. But it's not because I have some magical investment strategy to suggest. I am skeptical that you can beat the market. Market timers and sector rotators don't seem to succeed. The success rate appears to be slightly higher for folks who avoid big market calls and instead focus on picking stocks. But even there, the odds are heavily stacked against you. Most folks, I believe, would be well-advised just to buy a broad selection of stocks and then sit tight.

But if you do that, how are you going to outperform most stock-fund investors? The key is to stop fretting about performance and start focusing on costs. If, either directly or through funds, you own stocks whose results are close to the market averages, but you incur expenses that are much lower than those paid by most other investors, you should get superior results. Admittedly, you will still lag behind the market. But you won't lag by as much as other investors, so you will be ahead of the game. In effect, you win, but only by losing less. This, I readily concede, is hardly exciting stuff. But compared with the strategies suggested by the beat-the-market crowd, it's a much surer road to riches.

Intrigued? Here are five cost-cutting strategies.

Slash Your Commission Costs

If you go through a full-service broker, like one of the folks employed by Merrill Lynch & Co. or Smith Barney, you might pay $100 in commission to buy 100 shares. Interested in stock funds instead? A broker might snag 5.75 percent of your money for putting you in a fund, equal to $57.50 out of every $1,000 invested.

If this sounds steep, it is. But it doesn't have to be that way, thanks to no-commission mutual funds and discount brokers. Once one of the bigger costs for investors, commissions to trade individual stocks have come down sharply in recent years. If you shop around, you can find discount brokers that charge less than

$30 to trade individual stocks, while those willing to buy and sell through the Internet can cut their costs to less than $15 a transaction. Some companies, including Home Depot, Procter & Gamble and Wal-Mart Stores, will even sell their shares directly to investors, with little or nothing charged in the way of fees and commissions. Meanwhile, if your taste runs to mutual funds, there are plenty of decent "no-load" stock funds where there's no commission to either buy or sell.

Skimp on Mutual-Fund Expenses

Investors are rushing to dump individual stocks and buy funds instead. Yet mutual funds are, if anything, getting less attractive. The cost of buying and selling individual stocks is coming down, while the cost of owning mutual funds is rising. These days, diversified U.S. stock funds charge an average of 1.4 percent a year, equal to $1.40 for every $100 you have invested. Because of this 1.4 percent expense ratio, funds effectively have to earn 1.4 percent a year just to break even. What should you do? Stack the odds in your favor by sticking with no-load stock funds with low expenses, preferably below 1 percent a year.

Trade with Care

Many folks think the cost of trading individual stocks begins and ends with the brokerage commission. Not true. While you see only one price in the newspaper stock tables, every publicly traded company has two share prices, the bid and the ask. The asking price is the price you currently have to pay to buy shares. The bid price, which is always slightly lower, is the price that you would receive if you sold. The difference between the two is the so-called bid-ask spread and it represents the profit earned by the stock's market maker, the firm that brings buyers and sellers together.

With blue-chip stocks, the bid-ask spread is usually modest, maybe just 12½ cents, equal to 0.25 percent on a $50 stock. But if you trade the shares of smaller companies, the spread is often huge. With lower-priced stocks and thinly traded shares, the bid and ask prices might be 4 percent or 5 percent apart. With these stocks, you have to earn 4 percent or 5 percent just to break even. Indeed, you can easily lose more to the bid-ask spread than you pay in brokerage commissions to first buy and later sell the stock.

What to do? If you dabble in small companies, trade sparingly and carefully. For instance, when buying, don't just accept the current asking price. Instead, put in a limit order seeking to buy at a price below the current asking price. You might offer to buy at the current bid price or halfway between the bid and the ask. Sure, you would prefer to buy immediately and there's a chance your order won't get filled. But if you put in a lowball limit order and the trade is executed, you will have slashed your trading costs.

Watch for Account-Maintenance Fees

It used to be that brokerage firms would only charge you for trading. Now they also charge you just for being a customer. Account-maintenance fees are proliferating. Try to keep them to a minimum by limiting yourself to one brokerage account, or avoid them entirely by sticking with firms that don't charge these fees.

Ditto for the fees charged on mutual funds. Many fund companies will levy, say, a $12 annual fee if your account balance is below a specified minimum, plus maybe $10 for each individual retirement account. These fees usually get charged on each fund you own. Use that as an incentive to build up your accounts quickly and think long and hard before owning more than a couple of funds in your retirement account.

Stiff Uncle Sam

Taxes are the biggest investment cost of all. But you have two key defenses. One is retirement accounts. The other is sloth.

With retirement accounts, you get tax-deferred growth, which means you don't have to pay taxes on the investment gains you earn each year. Instead, any taxable gains aren't taxed until the money is withdrawn. How should you use retirement accounts? If you plan to trade frequently and will therefore be realizing your gains quickly, I would do this in your retirement account rather than your regular taxable account. By trading in your retirement account, you will also avoid the hassle of accounting for these transactions on your tax return each year. Similarly, if you plan to buy stocks with fat dividend yields, you may want to do so through a retirement account, where the dividends won't be immediately taxable.

For your taxable account, just the opposite applies. You should think twice about buying high-dividend-yielding securities, such as utilities and equity-income mutual funds, because you will have to pay income taxes on the dividends each year. Most critically, keep your trading to a minimum. Whether you are buying and selling in your taxable account or in your retirement account, less trading is generally better than more, because you avoid commissions and other trading costs. But minimizing your trades is especially important in your taxable account.

If you buy a stock in a taxable account and then hang on to it, you effectively get the same sort of tax-deferred growth that you would get by owning securities in a retirement account. How so? The capital-gains tax on any appreciation doesn't have to be paid until the stock is sold. By holding on to the stock and thus delaying the tax, you get to use the money for longer and thus you reap the benefit of any investment earnings generated by this money. Result? Your portfolio grows faster at the expense of Uncle Sam. It doesn't get much better than that.

MYTH NO. 6

YOUR INVESTMENTS WILL MAKE 10 PERCENT A YEAR

Call it the immaculate misconception.

You want to know how large your nest egg will be at retirement, so you buy one of those personal-finance software programs, such as Quicken or Managing Your Money or Microsoft Money. You take it home, load it on your computer, call up the program, plug in how much you have saved, how much you intend to save each year and when you plan to quit the work force. The program then tells you how much you will have upon retirement. But first you have to plug in one more number: your expected rate of return.

Welcome to Disney World for the post-teen set.

Many folks just assume they will make 10 percent, so that's the figure they plug in. The number, of course, has some basis in reality. Since year-end 1925, stocks—as measured by the Standard & Poor's 500-stock index—have returned 10.7 percent a year, according to Chicago researchers Ibbotson Associates. This 10 percent number has been tossed around so much that it is now firmly lodged in the public's consciousness. And 10 percent seems almost conservative, given the dazzling stock-market returns since 1982.

Where We Go Wrong

But what if you don't make 10 percent? What if you only make, say, 8.5 percent? Suppose you are 35 years old, you have $50,000 saved for retirement and you plan to sock away $4,000 every year between now and age 65. If you earn 10 percent a year, you will have $1.5 million at age 65. But if returns come in at 8.5 percent, you will retire with under $1.1 million, or 30 percent less.

A minor difference in your return can make a huge difference in the amount you accumulate for retirement, college and other goals. Clearly, the higher the return, the easier it is to meet your goals—and the less you need to save. On that score, making 10 percent would be nice. But you aren't likely to earn 10 percent a year over the long haul. You may not even come close. Why not? Here are four key reasons.

History May Be Bunk

The 10 percent figure is a seven-decade average. The returns in any one year, however, can be all over the map. Since World War II, stocks have gained as much as 52.6 percent in a single calendar year and lost as much as 26.5 percent. That 26.5 percent loss, in 1974, was preceded by a 14.7 percent drop in 1973, so that stocks lost a cumulative 37.2 percent in the two-year span. (The reason the two annual losses come to 37.2 percent—less than the two calendar-year numbers simply added together—has to do with the way investment compounding works. Because of the 14.7 percent loss suffered in 1973, an investor would have started 1974 with less money, which meant that year's 26.5 percent hit took its bite out of a smaller chunk, thus muting the dollar loss in the second year. A small consolation.)

You, of course, don't plan to invest for just one or two years.

You have 10 years to invest. Guess what? Between year-end 1964 and year-end 1974, which was the worst 10-calendar-year stretch for stocks since World War II, the S&P 500 gained just 1.2 percent a year. Once you start looking at 20-year and 30-year time periods, even the numbers for the worst stretches get closer to the long-run average. And, of course, you are less likely to get disastrous results if you diversify into foreign and small-company stocks and if you use dollar-cost averaging. But with all that, there's no guarantee that you will earn double-digit gains, particularly if you stick with stocks for only a few years.

It's All in the Mix

Even if stocks do deliver 10 percent, you are unlikely to pocket that much. How come? To get that sort of return, you really have to be 100 percent invested in stocks, which most of us aren't. Indeed, if you toted up all your investments and calculated the percentage that was in stock-market investments, you might well find that stocks account for less than half your portfolio. The rest is probably in bonds and cash investments such as money-market funds and certificates of deposit, which will drag down your returns over the long haul. In addition, you may find that your stock funds tend to hold 10 percent or more in cash and bonds, further boosting the percentage of your portfolio that is in more conservative investments.

Consider the Costs

Large-company stocks may have earned 10.7 percent a year since year-end 1925. But even if you owned every one of these stocks for the entire period, you wouldn't have earned 10.7 percent, thanks to investment costs. After brokerage commissions, mutual-fund expenses, trading spreads and account-maintenance fees have taken their toll, you might well find that your results are a percentage point or more below the market average. Once Uncle Sam gets his slice of your gains, your results would look even more grim.

Inflated Expectations

The 10 percent number is often quoted without mentioning that, since year-end 1925, inflation has run at 3.1 percent a year. Stock investors may have thought they were earning 10 percent. But after inflation, they were only pocketing 7 percent.

When you invest, it's not the nominal return that counts, but the real return—how much you have left after inflation has taken its bite. If we get double-digit annual inflation in the years ahead, you will be less than thrilled if your stocks deliver 10 percent. According to "Stocks for the Long Run" (Irwin, 1994) by Jeremy J. Siegel, a finance professor at the University of Pennsylvania's Wharton School, stocks have returned 6.7 percentage points a year above the inflation rate over the past 200 years. That's the sort of real rate of return—the return above inflation—that you should be looking for.

The New Rules

Thanks to the dazzling stock and bond returns of the 1980s and 1990s, many investors have a distorted idea not only of long-run stock-market performance, but also of likely gains from bond investing. But if anything, these recent stellar returns should prompt caution. The sparkling stock-market performance since August 1982 was preceded by a 16½-year stretch during which blue chips gained 5.1 percent a year, small stocks climbed 12.7 percent annually and foreign stocks returned an estimated 9 percent. These figures reflect both share-price changes and reinvested dividends. While I don't foresee blue chips reverting to 5 percent annual performance, I do suspect that future stock-market returns will come in much closer to the 10 percent a year historical average.

Many financial planners talk about "managing expectations." What do they mean by that? If their clients have unrealistic expectations about how much their investments will earn, they will inevitably be disappointed. But if their clients know what to expect, both in terms of likely short-term losses and probable long-run returns, they will have a more realistic idea of what they can achieve with their money and—if necessary—adjust the amount they save or the way they invest in order to reach their financial goals.

So if you are going to manage your own expectations, what sort of return should you anticipate making? Let's say you are trying to calculate the likely return on your retirement portfolio. Start by figuring out how your money is divvied up among stocks, bonds and cash investments. You might find that 50 percent of your money is in stocks, 25 percent is in bonds and 25 percent is in certificates of deposit, money-market funds and other cash investments.

To calculate the likely return on your bonds and bond funds, find out the current yield on the benchmark 30-year Treasury bond. Yield is only one component of a bond's return. Bonds also post price gains and losses. But over longer periods, the yield is by far the biggest component of an investor's return. The 30-year Treasury bond's yield is published every day in the business section of many newspapers. You should be able to find the number either among the financial data or in the daily market commentary. Is the yield on 30-year Treasuries a good indicator of future returns? It's close enough. If you own shorter-term government bonds, you will make somewhat less. On the other hand, if you invest in high-quality corporate bonds or high-yield junk bonds, your returns may be as good as, or better than, the current yield on 30-year Treasuries. Let's presume the 30-year Treasury number is 6.5 percent.

For your money-market funds, savings accounts, bank money-market accounts and certificates of deposit, simply look at the yield that these investments are currently paying and then calculate an average. If you have much of your cash in a savings account and shorter-term certificates of deposit, the number will be somewhat lower. If you own a money-market fund or longer-term certificates of deposit, the average will be somewhat higher. Let's say it's 4.5 percent.

What about your stocks? I would take the current inflation

rate and add seven. If inflation is running at 3 percent, you get a 10 percent return for your stocks. Using 10 percent for stocks, 6.5 percent for bonds and 4.5 percent for cash investments, you would then figure a weighted average for your portfolio, based on your mix of 50 percent stocks, 25 percent bonds and 25 percent cash. Thus, you multiply the 10 percent stock return by 0.5, the 6.5 percent bond return by 0.25 and the 4.5 percent cash return by 0.25, to get an average rate of return of 7.75 percent.

But what about investment costs? To adjust for these, I would take the 7.75 percent and knock off one percentage point, bringing your portfolio's return down to 6.75 percent. This one percentage point adjustment would be a little harsh if you were heavily invested in cash and a little lenient if you had much of your money in stocks or if you used a broker and did a lot of trading. But for a portfolio that's spread across stocks, bonds and cash, it's a reasonable number.

This one percentage point reduction for costs doesn't, of course, include taxes. But if you are saving for retirement, you are probably doing much of your investing through individual retirement accounts, your 401(k) plan or other retirement accounts that allow your money to grow tax-deferred. What about your investments in taxable accounts? Any dividends, interest and realized capital gains will be taxed each year. But if you're employed, you probably pay the tax on your investment gains out of your salary, rather than selling investments to meet the tax bill. Taxes

What If?   Want to figure out how much you might save for retirement, college and other goals? In addition to the many software programs available, there are also plenty of financial-planning tools offered on the Internet. Check out the financial calculators posted by Comfin (http://www.comfin.com), Fidelity Investments (http://www.fidelity.com), FinanCenter (http://www.financenter.com), T. Rowe Price Associates (http://www.troweprice.com), Quicken Financial Network (http://www.qfn.com) and Vanguard Group (http://www.vanguard.com).

may reduce your effective return, but they're not going to limit the growth of your existing investments, because you are paying Uncle Sam out of your income.

So back to the computer. You delete 10 percent and plug in 6.75 percent instead. With the new low number, your retirement kitty doesn't grow quite so impressively. Feel cheated? Want to kick the computer? It's better to know the bitter truth now, while you still have the chance to make up any shortfall by increasing the amount you save each month and maybe sticking more in stocks, so that you earn higher returns. Once you've made your initial projections for your own retirement, your kid's college and other goals, plan on firing up the computer every so often and checking your investment progress to make sure you are still on track. Who knows, you might even be pleasantly surprised.

YOU CAN'T GO WRONG
WITH MUTUAL FUNDS

In September 1988, while at *Forbes* magazine, I got promoted to staff writer and was given the job of writing about mutual funds. At the time, there weren't many reporters who wrote full-time about funds and it was widely derided as a boring and undesirable beat by my colleagues. Mutual funds themselves were treated with similar disdain by many on Wall Street. In 1988, the mutual-fund industry was halfway through its dozen-year transformation from sleepy backwater to Wall Street behemoth and the "smart money" crowd still looked upon funds as the preserve of the small—and hence, in their view, stupid—investor.

But I quickly came to like mutual funds. Indeed, I soon found I was both observer of the mutual-fund industry and cheerleader, scrutinizing funds not only to find stories, but also because I wanted to know how best to use these investments. Funds were easy to like. They had low investment minimums, sometimes only $500 or $1,000, which made them attractive to those on low salaries. Like reporters, for instance. They were easy to understand, so they appealed to folks who didn't know a lot about investing. Like reporters, for instance. And the investment costs involved were often low, so they attracted those who were tight with a buck. Like me, for instance.

As I reported on mutual funds and met mutual-fund managers and the executives who headed fund companies, I was surprised by how few came across as archetypal Wall Streeters. These folks didn't fit in New York. They weren't made to be fast-talking, foul-mouthed traders or hard-changing investment bankers, with slicked-back hair, suspenders and their egos worn on their sleeves.

Mutual funds were originally a Boston phenomenon. By the late 1980s, however, there were fund companies all over the country, in Chicago and Denver, in Baltimore and Kansas City, in Milwaukee and Minneapolis. But the fund-company employees still behaved as if they were from Boston. They talked about fiduciary responsibility and investor education and they acted as if they had a mission. They believed funds were the best bet for small investors and they were anxious to spread the message.

In early 1990, just as total mutual-fund assets were hitting $1 trillion, *The Wall Street Journal* offered me a job. Once there, I wrote exclusively about funds for a few years, before switching to the *Journal*'s "Heard on the Street" column and trying my hand at more general personal-finance pieces. Eventually I got my own column, which was dubbed "Getting Going" and which first appeared in October 1994. But even as I tackled other subjects, I kept coming back to funds. I liked mutual funds.

I don't like them so much anymore.

Where We Go Wrong

Why have I become so disgruntled with mutual funds? I have long been a fan of stock-market investing and I saw funds as the ideal vehicle for tapping the market. While dabbling in individual stocks was dicey, it seemed that—with a little bit of work—you really couldn't go too far wrong with stock funds. Lately, however, I have come to realize that the reality of fund investing just doesn't live up to the promise. How have stock funds failed? Consider:

Promise: A stock fund's portfolio manager will generate market-beating results.

Reality: Most stock funds fail to beat the market averages, usually lagging by about two percentage points a year.

Promise: Stock funds provide investors with a diversified portfolio of stocks, thus eliminating the risk that your portfolio will get badly hurt because one or two stocks or one or two market sectors get into trouble.

Reality: Some stock funds are so specialized that they are almost as risky as owning individual stocks.

Promise: Stock funds offer a low-budget way to invest in the market.

Reality: Many funds have boosted their investment minimums, thus freezing out investors with limited means.

You've Got to Start Somewhere

When I began investing, my appetite for mutual funds far outstripped my budget. I quickly ended up with too little money in too many funds and eventually sold many of them as I sought to simplify my finances. But along the way, I learned a lot about investing—including how you can get into many funds for far less than their stated investment minimum.

Unfortunately, in the years since I started investing, mutual-fund companies have made life increasingly difficult for low-budget investors. Gone are the days when most no-load funds had investment minimums of $1,000 and less. After the 1987 stock-market crash, many of the larger fund companies boosted their investment minimums to $2,500 and above, and others have followed suit in recent years. But even as the price of admission rises, there are still plenty of fine funds that you can buy for $1,000 or less.

The key is to be inventive. Starting small? Here's how to buy no-load funds if you are on a tight budget.

PAUPER'S FRIENDS

Some fund groups continue to have relatively low investment minimums for some or all of their funds. For instance, while Vanguard Group expects investors to pony up $3,000 for most of its funds, it allows shareholders to buy Vanguard Star Portfolio with just $1,000. Similarly, while it usually takes $1,000 or $2,500 to open an account at Strong Funds, you can get into Strong Asset Allocation Fund and Strong Total Return Fund for just $250.

The regular investment minimum remains $1,000 for some or all of the funds at Columbia Funds, Founders Funds, Gabelli Funds, Jones & Babson, Invesco Funds Group, Neuberger & Berman Management and Strong. Charles Schwab Corporation also imposes a $1,000 minimum for its own funds; the minimum for other companies' funds sold through Schwab's mutual-fund supermarket is $2,500 and up. Meanwhile, some of the AARP Investment Program funds, which are managed by the same folks who run Scudder Funds and which are open to investors who aren't members of the American Association of Retired Persons, have a low regular minimum of just $500. Babson Bond Portfolio Long, Babson Bond Portfolio Short, Babson Growth Fund, Nicholas Fund and Nicholas Income Fund also have regular $500 minimums.

OPEN AN IRA

If a fund has a prohibitively high investment minimum, see what it takes to open an individual retirement account. Many fund companies lower the hurdle for IRA investors. For instance, for $250, you can open a retirement account at no-load fund groups such as AARP, Invesco, Jones & Babson, Neuberger & Berman, Strong and USAA Investment Management.

Meanwhile, you need just $500 to set up an IRA at Fidelity Investments, Founders, Janus Funds, Stein Roe Mutual Funds and Warburg Pincus Funds. If you want to buy any of Schwab's own mutual funds, the minimum is also $500. Dreyfus Corporation expects IRA investors to ante up $750, while at American Century Investments, T. Rowe Price Associates, Scudder and Vanguard the minimum is $1,000.

DO IT REGULARLY

Many fund companies will eliminate or drastically reduce their investment minimum if you sign up for an automatic investment plan. With these plans, money is plucked out of your bank account or paycheck every month and deposited directly into a fund. To get the minimum waived or reduced, you usually have to agree to invest at least $50 or $100 every month. No-load fund companies offering this program include AARP, American Century, Columbia, Dreyfus, Founders, Gabelli, Invesco, Janus, Jones & Babson, Neuberger & Berman, T. Rowe Price, Strong and USAA.

CHILD'S PLAY

Funds will often cut their investment minimum if you set up a custodial account for a child. Parents flock to custodial accounts because the investment earnings generated by these accounts get a modest tax break. Custodial accounts, however, can also create major headaches because the money counts against you heavily when applying for college financial aid and because the child gets control of the account when he or she reaches the age of majority, usually 18 or 21, depending on the state.

But if you are determined to open a custodial account, fund companies sure make it easy. American Century, T. Rowe Price, Stein Roe and Vanguard allow you to open a custodial account with $1,000, while Founders, Janus, Schwab, USAA and Warburg expect $500. Fidelity also lowers the hurdle to $1,000, but its program only extends to five funds. Meanwhile, AARP, Jones & Babson, Neuberger & Berman and Strong let kids in for just $250.

Promise: Picking a top-notch stock fund is less time-consuming than putting together a portfolio of individual stocks.

Reality: With over 4,000 stock funds to choose from, and the number rising every day and the types of funds proliferating, selecting a stock fund takes almost as much research as picking an individual stock.

Promise: Stock funds are the cheapest way for small investors to tap the stock market.

Reality: Purchasing stock funds is often more costly than buying individual stocks, even if you avoid those funds that charge a sales commission. How come? Brokerage commissions to purchase individual stocks have dropped sharply in recent years, while stock-fund annual expenses have climbed.

The New Rules

But with all these flaws, you shouldn't give up on stock funds, because they can still be a great deal for the small investor. If you choose carefully, funds can provide you with a well-diversified portfolio of stocks at low cost, without all the accounting and paperwork hassles that you would suffer if you owned each stock individually. But these days, to find the right funds, you have to be much more selective. The fact is, there are probably fewer than 200 stock funds that you would really want to own.

How do you find these funds? Draw up a scouting list of funds that have intrigued you because you read about them in the press, saw an advertisement, heard about them from friends or spotted them at the top of one of the mutual-fund performance charts. Next, begin the process of elimination. With over 4,000 stock funds to choose from, you can afford to be picky. In fact, you have to be picky or you will be overwhelmed by the choice. When cutting down the list, the idea is to stack the odds in your favor, by eliminating stock funds that don't play a useful role in a well-diversified portfolio or that are so costly they are unlikely to perform well. From your scouting list, I would scratch all of the following funds.

Load Funds

Mutual-fund sales commissions are used to compensate brokers who sell funds. If you don't need a broker's advice, don't buy funds that charge sales commissions, also known as "loads" in mutual-fund lingo. By avoiding load funds, you will save yourself a bundle. Broker-sold funds can stiff you in three different ways, with a front-end load when you buy, with a back-end load when you sell and with a 12b-1 trail commission that nicks you for a little money every year that you are in the fund.

These days, most broker-sold funds charge a 12b-1 fee (so called because of the applicable Securities and Exchange Commission rule) in conjunction with either a front-end load or a back-end load. If a stock fund charges a front-end load, you will likely lose around 5.75 percent of the amount you invest to brokerage commissions. After that initial hit, the 12b-1 fee might snag 0.25 percent a year. Meanwhile, if the fund charges a back-end load, you will probably fork over 1 percent of your money each year to the trail commission, with the back-end load costing as much as 5 percent, if you cash out quickly.

Some funds will hit you with a front-end load, even if you don't use a broker. On this score, the biggest culprit is Fidelity Investments, which charges low-loads of 3 percent on many of its stock funds. Don't pay it. You can avoid most Fidelity loads by purchasing Fidelity funds in a retirement account rather than a regular taxable account. Looking to put some money in a taxable account? Stick with Fidelity's no-load stock funds or go elsewhere. It's tough to come out ahead in the investment game, so you sure don't want to be weighed down by unnecessary investment costs.

High-Expense Funds

All funds charge annual expenses, which pay for items like fund managers' salaries and shareholder servicing costs. With stock funds, these expenses typically run around 1.4 percent of assets a year, or $1.40 for every $100 invested. But this average disguises a huge range, with some funds levying less than 0.3 percent a year while others scalp investors for over 2 percent. Fund expenses have risen in recent years, partly because of the introduction of 12b-1 fees and partly because funds have boosted management fees.

But just as there's no need to pay mutual-fund loads, so it's easy to sidestep funds with high annual expenses. I would shoot to buy stock funds with annual expenses of below 1 percent. You may have to pay a little bit more for foreign-stock funds, small-company stock funds and emerging-markets funds. But even then, I wouldn't pay more than 1.5 percent a year, unless the fund has less than $100 million in assets and you can be confident that fund expenses will come down as the fund gets bigger.

High-Minimum Funds

If you aren't a high roller, you can safely ignore any fund with a minimum above $5,000. There's a growing group of funds that are geared toward institutional investors and wealthy individuals, and these funds just aren't interested in you or me. Occasionally, you can get into these funds for less than the minimum. A fund might lower or waive its minimum if you open an individual retirement account or set up an automatic investment plan, in which a fixed amount is transferred every month directly from your bank account or paycheck to the fund. But usually, if a fund has a really high minimum, it means it.

To find out a fund's investment minimum, as well as its sales commission, annual expenses and any other information you need, phone the fund involved and either talk to one of the telephone representatives or ask the fund to send you the latest prospectus and annual report. The prospectus is the fund's official sales document. While usually loaded with legalese, the prospectus does provide a lot of the basic fund information you need. Alternatively, to find this information, get hold of one of the comprehensive magazine mutual-fund surveys, such as those put out by *Barron's, Forbes, Kiplinger's Personal Finance* or *Money,* or pick up *The Wall Street Journal's* quarterly mutual-fund survey, which appears in early January, early April, early July and early October.

Global Funds

Global funds mix U.S. and foreign stocks in the same portfolio, while international funds invest exclusively abroad. I would

Call These Numbers for a Fund Time

Below are all of the major no-load fund families, plus some of the smaller groups, that offer funds with regular investment minimums of $5,000 or less. The amount shown for the typical fund investment minimum may not apply to all of the fund group's funds. Internet users who want more information on no-load funds might want to try the Mutual Fund Education Alliance (http://www.mfea.com).

Fund Group	Typical Minimum	Phone Number	Internet Address
AARP Investment	$2,000	800-322-2282	
Acorn Funds	1,000	800-922-6769	www.wanger.com
American Century	2,500	800-345-2021	www.americancentury.com
Artisan Funds	1,000	800-344-1770	
Baron Funds	2,000	800-992-2766	
Berger Associates	2,000	800-333-1001	www.bergerfunds.com
Bramwell Growth	1,000	800-272-6227	
Buffalo Group	2,500	800-492-8332	
CGM Funds	2,500	800-345-4048	cgmfunds.com
Clipper Fund	5,000	800-776-5033	
Columbia Funds	1,000	800-547-1707	columbiafunds.com
Crabbe Huson Funds	2,000	800-541-9732	www.contrarian.com
Dodge & Cox Funds	2,500	800-621-3979	
Dreyfus Corp.	2,500	800-645-6561	www.dreyfus.com
Fairmont Fund	1,000	800-262-9936	www.fairmontfund.com
Fasciano Fund	1,000	800-848-6050	
Fidelity Investments	2,500	800-544-8888	www.fidelity.com
First Eagle Funds	5,000	800-451-3623	
Flex-funds	2,500	800-325-3539	
Founders Funds	1,000	800-525-2440	www.founders.com
Fremont Mutual Funds	2,000	800-548-4539	
Gabelli Funds	1,000	800-422-3554	gabelli.com

Fund Group	Typical Minimum	Phone Number	Internet Address
Greenspring Fund	$2,000	800-366-3863	
Guinness Flight	5,000	800-915-6565	gffunds.com
Harbor Funds	2,000	800-422-1050	
Heartland Funds	1,000	800-432-7856	
Hotchkis & Wiley	5,000	800-346-7301	
IAI Mutual Funds	5,000	800-945-3863	networth.galt.com/iai
Invesco Funds Group	1,000	800-525-8085	www.invesco.com
Janus Funds	2,500	800-525-8983	janusfunds.com
Jones & Babson	1,000	800-422-2766	www.jbfunds.com
Kaufmann Fund	1,500	800-666-6151	www.kaufmann.com
Lexington Group	1,000	800-526-0056	www.lexingtonfunds.com
Lindner Funds	3,000	314-727-5305	www.lindnerfunds.com
Managers Funds	2,000	800-835-3879	
Marshall Funds	1,000	800-236-8560	www.marshallfunds.com
Meridian Funds	1,000	800-446-6662	
Monetta Funds	1,000	800-666-3882	
Montgomery Funds	1,000	800-572-3863	networth.galt.com/ montgomery
Mosaic Funds	2,500	800-336-3063	gitfunds.com
Nations Funds	1,000	800-321-7854	
Neuberger & Berman	1,000	800-877-9700	www.nbfunds.com
NI Funds	3,000	800-686-3742	
Nicholas Co.	500	800-227-5987	
Northeast Investors	1,000	800-225-6704	
Oakmark Funds	1,000	800-625-6275	
Oberweis Funds	1,000	800-323-6166	
L. Roy Papp & Assoc.	5,000	800-421-4004	
Pax World Fund	250	800-767-1729	paxfund.com
Payden & Rygel Funds	5,000	800-572-9336	
PBHG Funds	2,500	800-433-0051	www.pbhgfunds.com

Fund Group	Typical Minimum	Phone Number	Internet Address
T. Rowe Price Assoc.	$2,500	800-638-5660	www.troweprice.com
Reserve Funds	1,000	800-637-1700	www.reservefunds.com
Robertson Stephens	5,000	800-766-3863	www.rsim.com
Royce Funds	2,000	800-221-4268	www.roycefunds.com
Rushmore Group	2,500	800-621-7874	
Safeco Mutual Funds	1,000	800-426-6730	networth.galt.com/safeco
Schwab Funds	1,000	800-435-4000	www.schwab.com
Scudder Funds	2,500	800-225-2470	funds.scudder.com
Selected Funds	1,000	800-243-1575	
Sit Mutual Funds	2,000	800-332-5580	sitfunds.com
Skyline Funds	1,000	800-458-5222	
SSgA Funds	1,000	800-647-7327	
Stein Roe Funds	2,500	800-338-2550	www.steinroe.com
Strategist Funds	2,000	800-297-8800	americanexpress.com/direct
Strong Funds	1,000	800-368-1030	www.strong-funds.com
Third Avenue Funds	1,000	800-443-1021	mjwhitman.com
Transamerica Premier	1,000	800-892-7587	funds.transamerica.com
Tweedy Browne Funds	2,500	800-432-4789	
U.S. Global Investors	1,000	800-873-8637	www.usfunds.com
USAA Investment Mgmt	3,000	800-382-8722	
Value Line Funds	1,000	800-223-0818	
Van Wagoner Funds	1,000	800-228-2121	networth.galt.com/vanwagoner
Vanguard Group	3,000	800-662-7447	www.vanguard.com
Vontobel Funds	1,000	800-527-9500	
Warburg Pincus Funds	2,500	800-927-2874	
Wasatch Advisors	2,000	800-551-1700	

Fund Group	Typical Minimum	Phone Number	Internet Address
Westcore Funds	$1,000	800-392-2673	www.westcore.com
WPG Mutual Funds	2,500	800-223-3332	
Wright Mutual Funds	1,000	800-888-9471	
Yacktman Fund	2,500	800-525-8258	yacktman.com

stick with international funds. When you put $1,000 into an international fund, you know you are getting $1,000 of foreign stocks, or close to it. By contrast, with global funds, you can't be sure what your $1,000 is buying. You may have decided to put 20 percent or 30 percent of your stock-market money into foreign stocks. But your global-fund manager could mess up your portfolio, by making big shifts between U.S. and foreign shares. Global funds typically have two-thirds of their assets in foreign stocks and one-third in U.S. shares, but individual managers stray all over the map.

Regional Funds

Since the late 1980's, a rash of new funds have been introduced that stick with a single foreign region. These funds only invest in, say, Europe, or Asia, or Latin America, or Asia excluding Japan. Avoid them. When you invest in one of these regional funds, you are betting that one area of the world will perform better than others. But do you really know enough to make this sort of judgment? Professional money managers sometimes make these big bets and even they seem to be wrong as often as they are right.

If you are looking for foreign-stock exposure, my advice is to divide your money between two different types of funds, a diversified international-stock fund that invests in such developed markets as France, Germany and Japan and an emerging-markets fund that invests in developing economies such as Argentina,

Brazil, South Korea and Taiwan. By combining an international-stock fund with an emerging-markets fund, you will get broad stock-market exposure, you can control how much of your portfolio is in developed foreign markets and how much is in emerging markets and you do all this without buying a fistful of funds.

Sector Funds

Fidelity Investments, the country's largest fund company, introduced sector funds in 1981. Investors have been suffering ever since. Unfortunately, other fund companies have also entered the game, including Fidelity's archrival, Vanguard Group, which usually knows better than to introduce dumb funds.

Sector funds invest in a single industry sector, such as technology stocks, or health-care corporations, or gold-mining companies. Result? The funds can generate both awesome gains and astonishing losses. Often, they do so in quick succession. A fund shoots up the performance charts, investors pile in, the fund then falls out of bed and investors bail out, usually with less money than they started with. This happens with pathetic regularity.

Balanced Funds

For some investors, balanced funds are right up there with Mom, the flag and apple pie, as I discovered when I wrote a column for *The Wall Street Journal* arguing that these funds weren't a good investment. It was weeks before the hate mail stopped arriving.

Okay, balanced funds aren't a terrible idea. But you could do a lot better. Balanced funds divide their money between stocks and bonds, usually with 60 percent in stocks and 40 percent in bonds. They aim to provide one-stop shopping by offering a well-diversified portfolio in a single mutual fund. It's a nice idea, but balanced funds aren't the answer.

Why not? Here are four reasons. First, many balanced funds vary the percentage they hold in stocks and bonds, so you can never be sure what you are getting. Second, the bonds owned are usually taxable corporate and government bonds, but those in the

28 percent tax bracket and above would usually be better off own-ing tax-free municipal bonds. Third, the stock portion of the port-folio is typically invested in blue-chip stocks, so you don't get the diversification advantages of owning foreign shares and smaller companies. Fourth, many balanced funds have high expenses, es-pecially so when you consider that half the portfolio is invested in bonds.

My advice: If you want a balanced portfolio, build your own, mixing a variety of stock and bond funds. That way, you can di-versify your stock portfolio, you can own the sort of bonds that are appropriate for your tax bracket and you can determine how your money is divided between stocks and bonds.

Asset-Allocation Funds

This category includes two types of funds. One type you should avoid like the plague. The other is worth considering if you are a novice investor on a tight budget.

Many asset-allocation funds actively vary the mix of stocks, bonds and cash investments that they own, in an effort to catch rising markets and sidestep market declines. This, of course, is what market timers do. But market timing has fallen into disre-pute, so folks who make big market bets have taken to calling themselves tactical asset allocators. Like market timing, tactical asset allocation doesn't work, so skip these funds.

But don't write off the entire category, because some asset-allocation funds are worth owning. These more worthy funds aim to provide a diversified portfolio in a single fund, and they do so without making big market bets. Many fund groups now offer a series of three or four of these "lifecycle" funds. Within a series, each fund varies in aggressiveness, with maybe a conservative, a moderate-risk and a growth portfolio. But whatever their risk level, all of the funds tend to diversify across a host of stock and bond-market sectors.

I think lifecycle funds are a great idea. Indeed, for those who have limited money to invest and are looking for a fund that will provide one-stop shopping, I believe these funds are a better bet than traditional balanced funds, because lifecycle funds give you exposure to a broader collection of stocks and bonds. But before you buy a lifecycle fund, check carefully that you are getting a stable mix of stocks, bonds and cash and not some market-timing fund in drag.

So where do we stand? Gone are load funds, high-cost funds, high-minimum funds, global funds, regional funds, sector funds, balanced funds and most asset-allocation funds. If you use this elimination process, you will toss out the vast majority of stock funds. But you may still be left with a few hundred from which to choose. Still overwhelmed? Remember, we have rid ourselves of most funds and yet we haven't even considered one of the most critical factors in selecting stock funds. That factor, of course, is performance. That's the topic we tackle next.

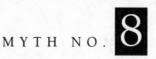

YOU CAN FIND
THE NEXT MAGELLAN

As manager of Fidelity Magellan Fund from 1977 to 1990, Peter Lynch made a lot of money for his shareholders. But he did a big disservice to everybody else.

How so? Lynch had an astonishing 13-year run as Magellan's manager, beating the market in every calendar year but two. He did so despite the fund's burgeoning size and despite predictions of failure from many observers, including me. Lynch gave hope to amateur investors, who had tried picking stocks themselves and failed. But now they had a new strategy. Instead of picking stocks, they would pick the managers who picked the stocks. Just as Lynch had proven his worth year after year, so there would be other Magellans that would provide investors with steady but stellar rocketship rides to wealth.

That, at least, was the theory. The reality? Every day, thousands of amateur investors, fund analysts, investment advisers, newsletter writers and financial journalists pore over the country's 4,000-plus stock funds, all looking to find the next Peter Lynch.

They are still looking.

Where We Go Wrong

Fidelity Magellan Fund finished the 1970s with one of the best records among diversified U.S. stock funds. It went on to even better things in the 1980s, finishing the decade as the mutual-fund industry's top performer. Lynch was treated like a rock star and Magellan came to epitomize the tremendous growth and huge success of the mutual-fund industry.

The 44 Wall Street Fund was also a dazzling performer in the 1970s, thanks to manager David Baker and his fondness for small, fast-growing technology companies. Indeed, in the 1970s, 44 Wall Street Fund generated even higher returns than Magellan and it ranked as the top-performing diversified U.S. stock fund.

But the 1980s weren't quite so kind to 44 Wall Street Fund's shareholders. The market for small technology stocks imploded, and so too did 44 Wall Street Fund. According to fund researcher Lipper Analytical Services, it ranked as the worst-performing fund in the 1980s, losing 73.1 percent. Past performance may be a guide to future results. But it's a mighty tough guide to read.

Fortunately, most stock funds don't self-destruct with quite the vigor of the 44 Wall Street Fund. Instead, "superstar" funds follow a rather predictable lifecycle. A new fund, or an old fund with a new manager, puts together a decent three-year or five-year record. A great feat? Hardly. Any half-decent, somewhat-disciplined manager should be able to string together a couple of good years once in a while. Investment styles go into and out of favor. If a manager specializes in, say, blue-chip growth stocks and he sticks with his niche, eventually these shares will catch the market's fancy and—providing the manager doesn't do anything too silly—three or four years of market-beating performance might follow.

Thanks to the market's fondness for blue-chip growth stocks, our blue-chip growth-stock fund pops up near the top of the three-year or five-year fund performance chart and a star is born. The media is quick to notice and the inevitable fund-manager profile follows, possibly in *Forbes* or *Money* or *Smart Money*. Unfortunately for the journalists involved, our fund manager is less interesting than most podiatrists. Surely, sir, you have an intriguing hobby? Maybe, sir, you could tell us an anecdote to illustrate your investment style? By the time the story reaches print, our fund manager comes across as wise and opinionated and insightful. The money starts rolling in and the fund's assets swell. That's when blue-chip growth stocks go out of favor. You can guess the rest.

Too harsh? Maybe I have seen too many "superstar" fund managers come and go. When they go, they tend to go gently into that good night, a performance whimper rather than a spectacular bust. I think of managers such as Gabelli Asset Fund's Mario Gabelli, Janus Fund's James Craig, Monetta Fund's Robert Bacarella, Parnassus Fund's Jerome Dodson, Pennsylvania Mutual Fund's Charles Royce, as well as Fidelity Asset Manager's former manager Bob Beckwitt and Fidelity Capital Appreciation Fund's former manager Tom Sweeney. None of these funds self-destructed, like 44 Wall Street Fund. But their managers had a hot streak and they attracted a lot of press attention and a lot of share-holder money, and then the hot streak turned tepid.

Investors who piled into these funds usually did okay, as long as they toughed it out and waited for the good times to re-turn. But many, of course, didn't stick around. They expected a glorious, heady whirlwind rush to riches. What they got was a lot of ups and downs. In the end, maybe shareholders earned returns that approached the market averages—providing they didn't buy just as performance was peaking and bail out after the first couple of rough years.

The New Rules

I think it is possible to identify winning stock-fund man-agers. But it's a lot more difficult than we are led to believe and I am not sure it is worth the effort. The odds are clearly stacked against you. Over a 10-year period, maybe only a quarter of diver-sified U.S. stock funds will beat the Standard & Poor's 500-stock index.

The Numbers Game

Put down that checkbook. Before you purchase any stock funds, decide how many you want to own. Why? It will determine what sort of funds you ought to buy. The more stock funds you buy, the more you can fine-tune your portfolio. But with every additional fund, you also increase the paperwork and accounting hassles.

So how many stock funds should you purchase? There isn't one right answer. A lot depends on how much money you have to invest and how interested you are in investing. One fund? Three funds? Six funds? Depending on how many stock funds you decide to buy, here are my suggested portfolio mixes:

■ If you buy just one fund, purchase a lifecycle fund.

■ If you purchase two stock funds, buy a broadly diversified U.S. stock fund and an international fund.

■ If you decide to put together a three-fund stock portfolio, buy a large-company stock fund, a smaller-company fund and an international fund.

■ If you opt for a four-fund portfolio, purchase a large-company growth fund, a large-company value fund, a smaller-company fund and an international fund.

■ If you are willing to purchase five stock funds, consider buying a blue-chip growth fund, a blue-chip value fund, a small-stock fund, an international fund and an emerging-markets fund.

■ If you settle on a six-fund portfolio, buy a large-company growth fund, a large-company value fund, a small-company growth fund, a small-company value fund, an international fund and an emerging-markets fund.

So if you are going to undertake the dubious endeavor of trying to identify star managers, what should you do? For starters, don't blindly buy funds based on past performance. Instead, before you even think about returns, I would use the elimination process described in Myth No. 7, throwing out all funds with high expenses, loads, an excessively narrow focus or an absurdly broad

Putting It All Together

How should you divvy up your money among the various stock funds you buy? Here's what a six-fund portfolio might look like:

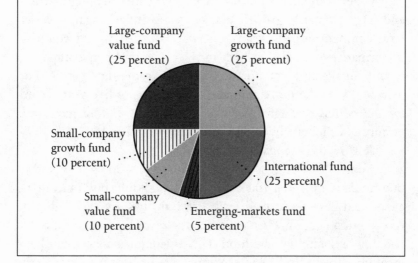

Large-company value fund (25 percent)

Large-company growth fund (25 percent)

Small-company growth fund (10 percent)

Small-company value fund (10 percent)

Emerging-markets fund (5 percent)

International fund (25 percent)

investment charter. Once you have gotten rid of all these funds, I would kick the tires on those funds that remain. Here are five questions to ask:

■ Does the fund make sense for your portfolio?

Most folks invest backward. They want to find top-performing funds, so they start by looking for stock funds with great records. But if you do that, you will be overwhelmed by the choice and end up with a mishmash of funds that, taken together, don't make any sense as a portfolio. Instead, you should start by deciding what sort of stock funds you want. That, in turn, depends on how many funds you are willing to buy. You might, for instance, opt for a six-fund portfolio, with a large-company growth fund, a large-company value fund, a small-company growth fund, a small-company value fund, an international fund and an emerging-markets fund.

Having settled on your mix, you then buy the best funds to fill each slot in your desired portfolio. How do you do that? Take the fund managers who intrigue you, divide them into categories based on the types of stocks they buy and then compare records. That way, small-stock value managers get stacked up against other small-stock value managers, emerging-markets specialists get compared to others who invest in emerging markets and large-company growth managers are judged against other large-company growth managers. If possible, I would compare performance over three, five and 10 years. When comparing records, make sure you are looking at the same time period. For instance, you shouldn't compare one manager's five-year record for the period through December 1997 with another manager's performance for the five years through November 1997.

■ How has the manager performed?

Funds don't pick stocks. Fund managers do. You shouldn't buy funds with stellar track records. You should buy fund managers who have performed well. If a fund has a great long-term record but a new, untested manager, the record is meaningless. By contrast, a spanking-new fund with a veteran manager can be a great investment. Indeed, these funds often perform spectacularly in their first year. The funds are relatively small, so their managers don't have to buy a lot of stocks and instead can concentrate their new fund's assets on their best stock-picking ideas.

If you are going to attempt to invest with the country's top fund managers, it's worth regularly reading your local newspaper's business section and one or two of the personal-finance magazines, so you hear about talented portfolio managers who start new funds or take over old funds with lackluster records. Once you have bought a fund, check every so often that the manager is still around. If the manager jumps ship, so should you, unless the fund brings in a new manager who also has a record of proven success.

■ What explains the manager's good performance?

You want to invest with managers who regularly beat the market by diligently picking one good stock after another. Look for fund managers who stick with either smaller or larger stocks, and then find winning securities by using a well-defined growth or value stock-picking method. Meanwhile, you want to avoid those who have scored big by switching between stocks and cash or by making hefty bets on one market sector after another. Why? While I have my doubts about any efforts to beat the market, it seems that a focus on stock picking holds out more hope than other methods. If a manager performs well by picking stocks carefully, he or she has made the right stock-picking decision on hundreds of occasions, thus suggesting a real skill. By contrast, managers who score big with market timing or sector rotating may have built their record on just half-a-dozen good calls. With such managers, it's much more difficult to say whether they are truly skillful or just unusually lucky.

How do you distinguish stock pickers from market timers and sector rotators? It's not easy. You may get some sense by reading the fund's most recent annual and semiannual report or by talking to one of the fund's telephone service representatives. But your best bet is to get your hands on *Morningstar Mutual Funds,* the premier mutual-fund newsletter (800-735-0700). At $425 a year, subscribing is a little too costly for most investors, so instead see if you can find *Morningstar* at your local library.

The Chicago newsletter offers detailed one-page analyses of some 1,700 stock and bond funds. Each page includes a mass of valuable information, such as annual expenses, loads, historical returns, the names of fund managers and how long they have held their jobs. Unlike other fund researchers, which divide funds into absurd categories like "aggressive growth," "growth and income" and "equity income," *Morningstar* divides stock funds based both on their stock-picking style (growth, value or a blend of growth and value) and on the size of the companies they own (small, medium or large). More critically, *Morningstar* also indicates whether funds have stuck with their particular niche. For those managers you are interested in, look at the historical style boxes, which show what sort of stocks the fund owned in each year. As with *Morningstar's* classification system, the style boxes tell you both the size of the companies bought and the stock-picking style. If a manager consistently falls in or close to the same style box, it's an indication that he or she sticks with a single sector of the market and a single investment style, and then aims to add value by picking the best stocks within that sector.

■ Has the manager performed consistently well?

Before you invest with any manager, look at his or her record on a year-by-year basis. By doing so, you can see whether the manager has performed consistently well or whether the record is really built on just one or two years of sizzling returns. Clearly, managers will have better absolute returns when all stocks do well and will look less good when the entire market struggles. What you want to avoid are managers who whip the market averages by a huge margin in one or two years and then perform at or below the market's return in other periods. This inconsistency suggests that the manager's record may be more the result of luck than skill.

■ Has the fund grown absurdly large?

If you want to understand one of the key problems with top-performing stock funds, just watch an ice-cream truck—reedy music blaring—drive down a suburban street on a summer day. Just as the neighborhood children can't stay away, so investors also swarm to top-performing funds. It's not a pretty sight. As investors pile into a top-ranked fund, its stellar returns inevitably dull, because the manager can no longer stick with his or her favorite stocks but instead must spread the fund's ballooning assets among a growing group of companies. This is a big problem and there's not a lot you can do about it. Your best bet is to buy funds before they get too large. Try to purchase small-company stock funds with assets of less than $500 million and large-company stock funds that have under $2 billion. What if the fund grows too big and returns turn rotten? Be prepared to bail out.

By asking the above five questions, you should be able to find funds that are brimming with promise. But the promise may never be fulfilled. This can be a tad disappointing if you made the mistake of becoming a shareholder. When do you decide that a talented manager has lost his or her touch? It can be an agonizing decision. As performance slows, you rack your brain. Is it merely that the manager's style is out of favor? Or has the fund grown too

Forget the Eggs, Enjoy the Omelet

When picking stock funds, a lot of folks pay attention to beta, standard deviation and other measures of individual fund risk. I wouldn't bother.

Sure, you might want to get a sense for how rough the ride has been, and that will give you a chance to consider whether the fund is too risky for your taste. But individual fund risk isn't that important. Instead, what really matters is your portfolio's risk level. That, in turn, depends not so much on individual fund risk, but on how you have your money divided among stocks, bonds and cash investments and on how well-diversified your stock portfolio is.

For instance, even if you own a couple of hard-charging growth-stock funds, you will still have a conservative portfolio if 90 percent of your money is sitting in a short-term bond fund. Similarly, emerging-markets funds are considered one of the most aggressive types of mutual funds you can buy. Indeed, if you looked only at individual fund risk, you would probably give them a miss. But a small stake in an emerging-markets fund—if it's part of a diversified stock portfolio—isn't going to boost your portfolio's risk level significantly and it may actually reduce it.

Keeping an eye on your portfolio's price swings—and ignoring individual fund returns—can also make you a more tenacious investor. If some of your funds take a dive and you feel queasy about how much you have lost, take a look at your portfolio's overall performance. Focus on the percentage decline, because this is usually less unnerving than contemplating the dollars lost. If you do the math, you will likely find that your fallen funds haven't put too much of a dent in your portfolio's overall value.

big? Could the fund manager's once-hot hand have turned permanently cold? Should you give the manager a year to turn it around, or two years, or three years? After you have stuck it out through three lean years, it's tough to call it quits, because you have seen enough rough years that you feel you deserve some good ones. Won't you feel like a chump if you bail out, only to find that the good performance immediately returns? What about the capital-gains taxes that will be due if you do sell? And so it goes on.

Here is what I would do. Before you dump a struggling fund, see if comparable funds are also lagging. You shouldn't worry if your small-company value fund is suffering along with other small-stock value funds. But if it's suffering alone and it does so for two consecutive years, ditch it. While you can never be entirely sure, the odds are you have bought yourself a lemon.

One more suggestion: If you are going to bet on the mutual-fund performance derby, I would do so in your retirement account. That way, if you do jump ship, you don't have to worry about the tax consequences. I would be inclined to invest through a major fund company, such as Fidelity Investments, T. Rowe Price Associates or Vanguard Group, where there are other good funds to switch into if you find yourself with a bum fund.

Alternatively, try one of the mutual-fund supermarkets, such as those offered by Fidelity Investments' Fidelity Brokerage Services, Charles Schwab Corporation and Jack White & Co. With these mutual-fund supermarkets, you can buy no-load funds from a host of fund groups. Sometimes, you have to pay a transaction fee to buy the funds in the supermarket. But often the fees are picked up by the funds themselves (which means, of course, that you pay indirectly, via the fund's annual expense ratio). The supermarkets make it easy to switch between funds. It's a convenience you may make ample use of as you try to keep your money invested with top-performing fund managers.

INDEX FUNDS ARE GUARANTEED MEDIOCRITY

Index funds are tough to get excited about. But I love them just the same.

These know-nothing, do-nothing funds don't try to beat the market. They simply buy the stocks that constitute an index in an effort to match the index's performance. Indeed, these funds don't even have fund managers, in the ordinary sense. The folks who run index funds don't bother distinguishing between the merits of different stocks. Instead, they devote their energies to ensuring that each of their funds tracks its designated index as closely as possible.

Index-fund managers do that by making sure their funds stay fully invested in stocks at all times and by keeping trading costs and other expenses to a bare minimum. If a fund tracks an index that includes a very large number of stocks, it may not buy every stock in the index and instead will use "sampling," which means the manager aims to buy a selection of stocks that will produce returns comparable to those of the entire index.

If all this sounds unexciting, it gets worse. Because index funds incur trading costs and because they charge annual mutual-fund expenses, they usually lag behind their benchmark index. When you buy an index, you are settling not merely for average results, but rather for less-than-average performance. Guaranteed mediocrity? It's undeniable. It turns out, however, that this guaranteed mediocrity is pretty darn good.

Yes, index funds will lag behind the market. But they will lag by only a fraction of a percentage point each year. Some of the lowest-cost index funds charge less than 0.3 percent a year in annual expenses and don't incur much in the way of brokerage commissions and trading costs, because they rarely buy and sell stocks. Meanwhile, active stock pickers and actively managed stock-mutual funds might lag by two percentage points a year, because their investment costs are so much greater and because actively managed funds typically hold 5 percent or 10 percent of their portfolio in cash, which acts as a drag on performance in rising markets. Index funds, by contrast, stay fully invested in stocks at all times. Like actively managed funds, index funds also lose ground to the market. But they lose by less than other funds, which makes them a winning investment.

Where We Go Wrong

The case for indexing is, I believe, utterly compelling. So how have investors responded? Most folks fall into two main camps. There are those who hate the idea of indexing and never do it. And then there are those who love the idea, but do it wrong.

Let's tackle the I-hate-indexing crowd first. Why the distaste for indexing? Contrary to what a lot of these folks believe, investing is not a game and, if it is a game, it is certainly not a game that you are likely to win. Investing is not about proving that you are smarter or more macho than everybody else. It's not about having something to brag about at the office water cooler or at your next cocktail party. Hubris is rarely rewarded on Wall Street. "If you don't know who you are, the stock market is an expensive place to find out," quipped George Goodman, who is best known as the host of *Adam Smith's Money World,* the well-regarded television business show.

Investing can be fun, but it's also a serious undertaking, with lots at stake. Investing is about making sure you have enough money to buy a decent house, put your kids through college and retire in comfort. So when you invest, you should try to be as rational as possible.

Standing here on my soapbox for the last 25,000 words or so, I have tried to prod you to rethink your financial strategies by ripping apart some of the great investment myths, including beliefs that you can beat the market, that you can find winning stocks, that you can pick top-notch mutual funds and that your biggest worry should be short-term market fluctuations. Along the way, I have tried to hammer home five key points:

■ If you are a long-term investor, your greatest enemies are inflation and taxes, not short-term market fluctuations.

■ Your asset allocation—how you divvy up your money among stocks, bonds and cash investments—is the key determinant of your long-run investment performance. The more you have in stocks, the higher your long-run investment returns and thus the wider the margin by which you will outpace inflation and taxes.

■ If you want to ensure that you get the benefits of stock-market investing, you have to diversify widely by owning a broad collection of blue-chip, small-company and foreign stocks.

■ It's tough to beat the stock-market averages by sector rotating, market timing or picking stocks. These strategies fail because you can end up in the wrong part of the market at the wrong time, because you are competing for investment gains against other investors who are at least as savvy and because you incur investment costs.

■ Because of the burden of investment costs, most investors will not beat the market. In fact, you are likely to lag behind the market averages, possibly by two percentage points a year or more.

What should you make of these five points? If you are a

long-term investor, you want to be in stocks, you want to be broadly diversified and you want to keep investment costs to a bare minimum. What's the best way to do that? Index funds. Sure, if you manage your portfolio actively and you beat the market by half a percentage point a year, that would be an astonishing achievement and you would find it easier to meet your financial goals. But if you buy index funds and merely earn returns that match the market averages, you will also do very nicely—and a lot better than most other investors.

For me, the biggest risk isn't being in the market and suffering all the daily turmoil. Rather, for me, the biggest risk is being in the stock market and not getting rewarded for my pains, because I don't earn stock-market returns. I am confident I will be able to retire in comfort and put my kids through college, just as long as I save regularly and earn results that rival those of the stock-market averages. On that score, index funds offer a degree of certainty that you don't get with other stock-market strategies. With any stock-market investment, you don't know what your returns will be from year to year. But with index funds, you do at least know that you will get results that are pretty close to the stock-market averages. Indeed, because indexing removes one of the great uncertainties—how an investor will fare relative to the market averages—I find I am willing to invest even more in stocks, thus further boosting my returns.

Sound attractive? Unfortunately, even those who come to see the virtues of indexing end up making a fundamental mistake. When they index, all they do is buy a fund that mimics the Standard & Poor's 500-stock index. These funds, of course, are the most visible indexing successes. Vanguard Group introduced the first S&P 500 index fund for small investors in 1976. The astonishing success of that fund, which has regularly beaten most actively managed stock funds, has spurred many fund groups to introduce S&P 500 funds of their own.

The problem is, when you buy an S&P 500 fund, you are not indexing the stock market. All you are doing is indexing 500 blue-chip stocks. These stocks have performed astonishingly well through the 1980s and 1990s. But what if, going forward, they lag badly while smaller stocks and foreign shares sparkle? At that point, of course, S&P 500 funds won't look so great and many investors will no doubt dump their funds in disgust and dismiss the whole notion of indexing. But the problem won't be indexing. Instead, the problem is that these folks never indexed properly.

The New Rules

So how should you go about indexing? You don't want to index just the S&P 500. Instead, you want to index the world, hitting all of the big three sectors, blue-chip stocks, small-company stocks and foreign stocks. With blue-chip and small-company stocks, you want to own them in proportion to their importance in the U.S. stock market, which means having roughly two dollars in smaller stocks for every five dollars you have in the S&P 500. What about foreign shares? If you owned them in proportion to their importance in the global stock market, you would end up with 57 percent of your money abroad. But that's far more money in foreign stocks than you need to get decent diversification. Indeed, if you put 57 percent of your stock-market portfolio into foreign shares, your overall portfolio would suffer some unnecessarily wild price gyrations. Instead, to get the diversification advantage, I would shoot for 20 percent or 30 percent of your stock-market portfolio in foreign stocks.

If you want to build this sort of portfolio, your best bet is to use the index funds offered by either Charles Schwab Corporation or Vanguard Group. Schwab offers a variety of index funds, all with $1,000 minimums. I would combine Schwab 1000 Fund (which owns the 1,000 largest U.S. companies, based on stock-market capitalization), Schwab Small Cap Index Fund (which invests in the second 1,000 largest U.S. companies) and Schwab International Index Fund (which buys the 350 largest publicly traded foreign companies).

Schwab's funds are managed with an eye to minimizing each fund's annual capital-gains distribution. This is helpful for taxable shareholders, who would otherwise have to pay taxes on these

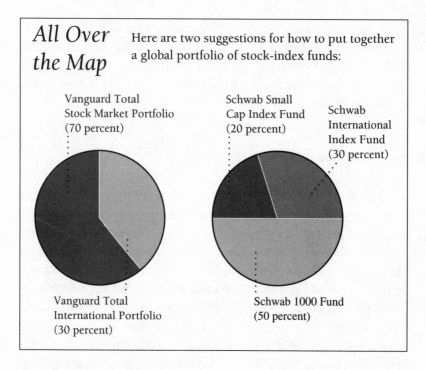

All Over the Map

Here are two suggestions for how to put together a global portfolio of stock-index funds:

Vanguard Total Stock Market Portfolio (70 percent)

Schwab Small Cap Index Fund (20 percent)

Schwab International Index Fund (30 percent)

Vanguard Total International Portfolio (30 percent)

Schwab 1000 Fund (50 percent)

distributions, even if they chose to reinvest the money in additional fund shares. But despite this tax advantage, I favor Vanguard's index funds. How come? Schwab's expenses may be low, but Vanguard's funds are unbeatably thrifty.

Vanguard offers a host of index funds, most of which have $3,000 minimums. Some of these index funds buy just smaller companies, or just emerging markets, or just European stocks, or just blue-chip growth stocks. The Valley Forge, Pennsylvania, fund group even has funds that index the bond market. Vanguard also makes heavy use of indexing in its four lifecycle funds, which are a good choice for small investors looking for a diversified portfolio in a single mutual fund.

But my two favorite Vanguard index funds are the Total Stock Market Portfolio, which indexes the entire U.S. stock market, and the Total International Portfolio, which indexes European, Pacific and emerging-markets securities. By combining these two funds, you can get broad global diversification at rock-bottom expense—and the guarantee that you will do better than the vast majority of stock investors.

You still prefer actively managed stock funds? Consider constructing two parallel stock portfolios. Put together a global portfolio of actively managed stock funds in your retirement account and then build a global portfolio of index funds in your taxable account, using either Vanguard or Schwab's funds. As I suggested in Myth No. 8, retirement accounts are the best place to buy actively managed stock funds. If you have to sell a fund held in your retirement account because the manager leaves or the fund's performance turns tepid, you won't have any tax bills or tax hassles.

Meanwhile, use your taxable account to buy index funds. I believe index funds make sense for any stock-market money, whether it's in your retirement account or your taxable account. But the case is especially compelling for taxable-account money. On top of all their other advantages, index funds are extremely tax-efficient. Because these funds rarely sell stocks, they don't make large capital-gains distributions each year. And because index funds aren't actively managed and don't have real portfolio managers, you will never have to sell an index fund because the manager leaves or because the performance starts badly trailing the market averages. These problems just aren't going to arise.

My advice? Forget about actively managed funds. Forget the mutual-fund performance derby. Forget about beating the market. Instead, buy index funds and you'll never have to say you're sorry.

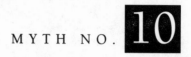

NOTHING'S SAFER THAN MONEY IN THE BANK

Most bank branches aren't particularly grand anymore. The marble pillars and magnificent lobbies are gone, replaced by the grim austerity of pared-down, strip-mall minimalism. But who needs to go in? The automatic teller machine outside will suck in your deposit and spit out your cash, long after the real tellers have gone home.

Yet even as banking degenerates into drive-through fast food, many Americans remain hopelessly hooked. Banks still symbolize all that can be secure and comforting about money. They aren't some mutual fund at the end of a toll-free telephone line or a brokerage account that exists only on a monthly statement. With bank accounts, there are no unnerving share-price swings and usually no tricky questions of credit quality.

Rather, banks are the epitome of financial prudence and permanence. Unless you withdraw money, your savings accounts, certificates of deposit and bank money-market accounts will only grow, not shrink. Bank accounts are insured by the Federal Deposit Insurance Corporation. Banks do sensible things, such as lend money to home buyers and help with second mortgages. Yes, ladies and gentlemen, banks are safe—just so long as you don't mind losing money.

Where We Go Wrong

If you want insurance, you would probably see an insurance agent. If you are in the market for stocks and bonds, you would go to a brokerage firm. If you are interested in funds, you might call a mutual-fund company. So as an investor, why would you go into a bank? To get cash investments, such as savings accounts, bank money-market accounts and certificates of deposit.

Cash investments can play a critical role in your portfolio. True, the long-run return on cash investments is dreadful. But cash has a number of appealing attributes. Among the big three financial assets—cash, bonds and stocks—cash is the only one that doesn't fluctuate in value. If you need to tap your portfolio on short notice, your bonds may be deeply underwater and your stocks may be suffering mightily. But your cash won't ever fall in value, so there's never a bad time to sell. Moreover, when you do sell cash, there are no tax hassles. You won't ever have a capital gain or loss, so there are no messy accounting problems when it comes time to fill in your tax return.

But cash shouldn't be thought of as an isolated investment. Instead, you should view it as a complement to your stock portfolio. Ditto for bonds and other investments. Stocks are your portfolio's engine of growth. Everything else is there to reduce risk, so that you won't get unnerved by market swings and can tap your portfolio for spending money without selling stocks at fire-sale prices.

If you are looking to provide some ballast for your stock portfolio, I believe cash is a better bet than most types of bonds. Why? Over the past two decades, stocks have become increasingly sensitive to interest rates. Result? When rates rise, both stocks and bonds tend to tumble at the same time. Meanwhile, if interest rates climb, cash performs well because the rising rates drive up the yield on cash. Indeed, while cash may not generate long-run returns that outpace inflation and taxes, it is in many ways the perfect short-run inflation hedge. As inflation rises, so too will interest rates, and this gets reflected immediately in the yield offered by cash investments. Because cash performs well at times of rising rates and accelerating inflation, it provides a much better cushion for a stock portfolio than most bonds.

Cash investments, however, won't do quite as well as bonds during a recession. If economic growth slows, stocks will probably drop and interest rates will likely decline. Those falling interest rates will help bonds by driving bond prices higher. But cash investments will be hurt as yields get squeezed. Even with their shrunken yields, however, cash investments will still provide some ballast for your stock portfolio.

Starting to feel fondly toward bank certificates of deposit and savings accounts? There's just one problem. Banks are a lousy place to buy cash investments because the yields offered are so low. Indeed, if you want to get robbed, simply put your money in a bank, that haven of safety so beloved by your parents and your friends and your colleagues. The math is simple enough: Your savings account earns 2.5 percent, which—if you are in the 28 percent tax bracket—gets sliced down to 1.8 percent after taxes have taken their toll. Then inflation steals 3 percent. Result? Every year, your money loses over 1 percent of its value.

Because of the twin threats of inflation and taxes, banks turn out to be one of the most perilous places possible to keep your savings. By putting your cash in the bank, you are pretty much guaranteeing that you will lose money. Couldn't banks cough up a little bit more in interest? Not really. Banks come burdened with huge overhead, which makes it tough for them to offer competitive yields. All those bank branches—even the scuzzy ones in strip malls—have to be paid for. Most mutual-fund companies, meanwhile, don't have anything more than a single building and a few telephone lines. Is it any wonder that funds offer decent returns, while banks are forced to steal you blind?

Yet the lambs line up for the slaughter. An astonishing amount of money languishes in low-yield savings accounts and no-yield checking accounts. Why do folks keep thousands and thousands of dollars in these accounts? What disaster are they expecting? What keeps them from buying other, better-returning investments? Do they mind that the value of their money shrinks with every passing year? I find the fondness for banks utterly bizarre.

It's time to wise up. Forget savings accounts. Forget bank money-market accounts. Forget short-term certificates of deposit. All three of these cash investments offer miserable yields. Also forget about longer-term certificates of deposit. They may offer higher payouts. But longer-term CDs lock in yields and lock up your money, which is not what you want from a cash investment.

You should keep enough money in a checking account to avoid banking charges, and that's it. What if you have additional cash that you want to invest? Get smart. Take the money out of the bank.

The New Rules

So where should you invest your cash holdings? Start by considering a money-market mutual fund. It still won't make you a lot of money. But the risk is minimal and the performance should be a lot better than that of a savings account.

Money funds seek to maintain a stable share price, usually pegged at one dollar, by buying Treasury bills, short-term municipal and government agency debt and the short-term corporate IOUs known as commercial paper. By law, the securities owned by money funds must, on average, mature within less than 90 days. Since they were introduced in 1971, only two money-market funds have "broken the buck" by allowing their share price to fall permanently below one dollar. The more recent victim—Community Bankers U.S. Government Money Market Fund, a fund geared toward institutional investors—broke the buck in 1994. The other fund, First Multifund for Daily Income, got into trouble in late 1978. But First Multifund, which owned securities with an average maturity of almost two years, wouldn't even qualify as a money-market fund today. In the 1990s, a number of money-market funds have had problems with their commercial paper, but avoided dropping below the one-dollar share price by selling the troubled securities to the fund's investment adviser. The investment adviser then ate the loss.

But even if some of your money-market fund's holdings got into trouble and the investment adviser didn't bail out the fund, the loss would likely be minimal and you would still end up with better results than those who stuck with savings accounts and their ilk. When picking a money-market fund, look for those that have over $1 billion in assets and are offered by major fund companies and brokerage firms. These funds should be well-diversified and well-managed, and the investment advisers are more likely to bail out the fund if one of its securities gets into trouble. Most critically, stick with funds that have low annual expenses, preferably below 0.6 percent a year. These expenses come straight out of the yield, so the lower the expenses, the higher your return.

Most money-market funds invest largely in corporate commercial paper and government debt. These funds are the best bet for most investors. Some funds only buy Treasury bills. That may appeal to the ultra-conservative, but it seems to me to take caution to excess. More intriguing are tax-exempt money-market funds, which stick with municipal securities and pay dividends that are exempt from federal taxes and, in some cases, state and local taxes as well. These funds may make sense for those in the 28 percent tax bracket and above.

Money-market funds offer everything you would want in a cash investment. Yields respond rapidly to changes in short-term interest rates. You have easy access to your money. When you want to tap your cash hoard, all you do is write a check. Because money-market funds seek to maintain a stable one-dollar share price, you shouldn't ever have a capital gain or loss, so writing checks doesn't lead to any messy tax accounting. But don't get too excited. Money-market funds won't make you rich. They just happen to perform better than the dismal alternatives offered by your local bank.

What if you want even higher returns on your cash? If you

are willing to endure a tad more risk and a few more hassles, you could put some of your cash in a no-load short-term bond fund. These funds, which hold bonds with two or three years to maturity, might return 1.5 percentage points a year more than a money-market fund. But there's a chance of modest short-term losses, which can be upsetting if you have to dip into your cash hoard. And if you dip too often, you can get into some messy tax reporting. Just as mutual-fund companies let you write checks against your money-market fund, so they will give you a checkbook when you open an account for a short-term bond fund. The problem is, every time you write a check against your short-term bond fund, you realize a capital gain or loss, which then has to be reported on your tax return. Take my advice: Burn the checkbook.

IF YOU NEED INCOME, BUY BONDS

Investors love bonds. It's what you would call a sado-masochistic relationship. Bonds suck investors in with their fat yields, then bludgeon them with inflation, taxes, defaults, early redemptions and more. Yet folks keep coming back for more.

Is this sick or what? What it is, of course, is the power of a well-entrenched financial myth. If you want income, you buy bonds. Isn't that what your parents told you? Even today, the advice seems eminently sensible. Bonds, after all, kick off far more immediate income than the other two financial assets, stocks and cash investments. Moreover, not only do you get the fat yield, but you also get safety of principal. You fork over your money to the bond's issuer, who pays you interest every year until the bond matures, at which point you get your money back. Which is what your parents also told you to do. Remember? Never dip into capital, they counseled. Only spend income, they said. Bonds are a prudent investment, they told you.

What do I think? I think bonds stink. They make a craven appeal to our worst instincts and then hit us hard when we least expect it. Folks whine that stocks are risky. But believe me, bonds can be just as bad.

Where We Go Wrong

How bad are bonds? Consider:

■ Bonds can be ravaged by inflation. Much trouble stems from the widespread belief that, if you spend your yield but never dip into your principal, you have protected your capital. Indeed, this is a favorite tactic of retirees. They buy bonds, spend the interest and then, whenever one of their bonds matures, they roll the proceeds into a new bond and start spending the interest from that bond. A good strategy? Get real.

Suppose you buy a 10-year bond and try to live off the interest. What happens? Your annual income is almost guaranteed to shrivel. Even at a modest 3 percent inflation rate, the spending power of both your interest payments and the bond's par value will be cut by 26 percent after 10 years. To fend off the threat from inflation, you really need to save some of the interest you earn each year and reinvest it in your portfolio, so that your portfolio's value keeps growing along with inflation. That, of course, means there's less money to spend.

So what sort of returns can you expect from bonds, after making allowances for inflation? Over the past seven decades, longer-term government bonds have delivered just 1.9 percentage points a year more than inflation, according to Ibbotson Associates. But it shouldn't be quite so bad going forward. Bonds were hijacked by the inflationary surge of the late 1960s and 1970s. Now investors are more leery. These days, many experts look for the benchmark 30-year Treasury bond to yield at least three percentage points a year more than inflation. That three percentage points, while higher than the historical average, is still far less than the seven percentage points a year above inflation that's expected from stocks.

■ Bonds can be rocked by interest-rate increases. If inflation spikes up, for instance, investors will demand that new bonds that are brought to market pay interest rates that offer a premium over the new expected inflation rate. That may be good news for current bond buyers, but it's bad news if you own existing bonds. You are locked into a low yield and your bond's price will fall to reflect that. Existing bonds and interest rates move in opposite directions. When interest rates rise, bonds sink. When interest rates fall, bonds soar. The further a bond is from maturity, the bigger the price swings.

Indeed, longer-term bonds can be almost as volatile as stocks. These price fluctuations aren't an issue if you buy an individual bond and hold it to maturity. But all the gyrations could prove costly if you have to bail out of your bonds before they mature. Rising interest rates could drive your bonds below your purchase price, forcing you to take a loss if you decide to sell.

■ If you bail out of your bonds before they mature, not only might you lose money, but you also have to contend with the perils of the secondary market. The bond market is geared toward institutional money managers, not small investors. There's no central marketplace, as there is for stocks, so it's tough to know whether you are getting a decent price when you buy or sell.

Part of the problem is that there are just so many bond issues available. A company will probably have just one class of shares outstanding. But it might have issued half a dozen or more different bonds, each of which trades separately. Add to this all the different government, mortgage and municipal bond issues and you find there are almost five million securities sloshing around the U.S. bond market. By contrast, there are only some 11,000 stocks listed on the New York Stock Exchange, American Stock Exchange and Nasdaq Stock Market. Many bond issues are small and trade infrequently, making prices difficult to obtain. Not surprisingly, once you get outside the big, liquid issues, selling can be tricky. Even if you find a dealer who is willing to buy your bonds, you may get offered a lousy price. The dealer is used to handling professional money managers with millions to invest. Your $10,000 bond just doesn't command a lot of respect.

■ Adding bonds doesn't reliably reduce a portfolio's risk level. As I have mentioned before, stocks should be your core investment. Everything else is thrown in to calm your port-folio and make it easier to tap your investments for income. When it comes to reducing risk in a stock portfolio, most bonds—through no fault of their own—often fail. Over the past two decades, stocks have become increasingly sensitive to changes in interest rates, which means they behave more like bonds. Result? When interest rates rise, both stocks and bonds will sink together.

Of course, stocks sometimes fall for reasons other than rising interest rates, so bonds won't always let you down. For instance, if the economy is slipping into recession and investors are worried about corporate earnings growth, stocks will fall but bonds should at least tread water and they will probably rise, thus helping to offset your stock-market losses. Thus, bonds will sometimes act as a shock absorber for your stocks. But they don't provide reliable portfolio protection.

■ Investors may like bonds, but the tax man likes them even more. While you might be fortunate enough to earn some capital gains with your bonds, the bulk of your return takes the form of yield. All of this yield is immediately taxable as ordinary income, unless you own municipal bonds or hold your bonds in a retirement account. Owning taxable bonds can prove especially punishing for those in higher tax brackets. Thanks to the 1997 tax bill, capital gains are now taxed at no more than 20 percent, so long as the investment is held for at least 18 months. But the tax on income, including the income from bonds, can run as high as 39.6 percent.

■ Corporate and municipal bonds can be paid off early by their issuers. Typically, these bonds are callable 10 years after they were first sold. You may have astutely bought bonds when interest rates were at historic highs and watched with pleasure as interest rates drifted lower. Your pleasure, however, may not last. Using the bonds' call provision, the issuer can steal back your bonds and then, in all likelihood, refinance this debt at lower interest rates. What if interest rates rise, rather than fall? The issuer won't call the bonds and you are stuck with low-yielding securities. For the issuer, it's heads I win, tails you lose.

Mortgage bonds, which are bonds backed by home mortgages, effectively work the same way. When interest rates fall, homeowners rush to refinance their mortgages, which means owners of mortgage bonds get early repayment of part of the bond's principal value. What if interest rates rise instead? Homeowners don't refinance and investors are saddled with low-yielding mortgage bonds.

■ Bond holders suffer so-called reinvestment risk. If your bonds get called in before maturity or you get early principal payments on your mortgage bonds, you may want to plow the money back into new bonds. But interest rates may have fallen, so that the new bonds you buy yield far less than those you previously owned. The same thing can happen if you reinvest your regular

---

The Bonds That Gag

Okay, so bonds stink. How about bond funds instead? Hard as it is to imagine, bonds funds are even worse.

Admittedly, funds offer some advantages. No-load bond funds are a lot easier and cheaper to sell than individual securities, and they provide a number of useful services. You can reinvest your dividends, so that your dividends automatically buy additional fund shares. Bond funds are also more accessible to small investors. If you dabble in individual municipal or corporate bonds, you really need $50,000 or $60,000, so that you can reduce the risk of default by spreading your money among five or six issues. By contrast, the minimum needed to buy a bond fund may be only $1,000 or $3,000, and you can subsequently add to your account with as little as $50 or $100.

Seem attractive? Unfortunately, the advantages offered by funds come with a steep price tag. In particular, bond funds have two major drawbacks.

The first drawback is that many funds are horribly expensive.

You may avoid sales commissions by sticking with no-load bond funds, but you still get hit with the fund's annual expenses. These expenses are gradually deducted from a fund's dividend payments, thus reducing its yield. Because of these costs, most bond funds lag behind their benchmark index, just like stock funds. Bonds funds levy annual expenses of around 1 percent on average. If you are purchasing a high-quality corporate, municipal or government bond fund, I would aim to buy funds that charge less than 0.7 percent a year. You may have to pay slightly more if you want a high-yield junk-bond fund, a foreign-bond fund or an emerging-market debt fund. But even for these funds, I wouldn't fork over more than 1.2 percent a year.

If you are looking for low-cost bond funds, Vanguard Group is often the best bet. But Vanguard doesn't offer some of the more exotic varieties of bond funds, such as foreign-bond funds or emerging-market debt funds, so you will have to go elsewhere for those.

Because mutual funds tend to be expensive, don't rule out individual securities when investing in Treasury, municipal or top-quality corporate bonds. If you buy individual bonds when they are first issued and hold them to maturity, you may be able to avoid commissions, and you don't face the pitfalls of the secondary market. In particular, consider buying Treasury bonds directly from the Federal Reserve, thereby saving on commissions and avoiding the hassles of trading in the open market. To find out more about the Treasury Direct program, contact your local Federal Reserve bank or branch or call the Bureau of the Public Debt at 202-874-4000. Treasuries are an especially good choice for smaller investors, because there's no risk of default and thus you don't have to worry about buying a slew of issues to build a diversified portfolio.

The second major drawback? Individual bonds mature. Most bond funds never do. Result? Suppose you are saving for a house, which you plan to buy in five years. If you can buy a high-quality bond that's unlikely to be called early and that has five years to maturity, you will have a very good idea of what your investment gain will be over the next five years. You know how much you will receive in interest each year and you know how much you will get back when the bond matures.

But if, instead of buying a five-year bond, you purchase a shorter-term bond fund that aims to hold five-year bonds, much of this certainty disappears. The fund's manager will tinker constantly with the portfolio, buying and selling securities so that the fund maintains its five-year maturity target. As a result, you can never be sure how much you will get in interest each year, and you don't know how much you will get back when you sell your fund shares. In effect, by taking bonds and sticking them in a fund, you bring about a bizarre transformation. You strip away the element of certainty, thereby sacrificing one of the few benefits of bond investing. Wine into water, anyone?

interest payments. When you buy additional bonds—or additional shares of a bond mutual fund—you may well find that your money buys bonds with a far lower interest rate.

■ Last but not least, there's always the risk of default. This isn't a problem with Treasury bonds. But if you buy municipal and corporate securities, it pays to be cautious. The biggest risk is with high-yield junk bonds and the mutual funds that own them. Investors were badly burned in the 1989–90 junk-bond debacle, when many heavily indebted companies got their first taste of recession and quickly discovered that the company's cash flow couldn't possibly cover the interest due on the bonds.

The New Rules

Yet with all these problems, investors continue to flock to bonds and bond funds. I blame our fetish for yield. Investors like the idea that the bulk of their annual investment return comes in the form of a fat, reliable check. They feel they are being prudent, because they can spend the interest while knowing that their principal is still intact. For many investors, who are trying to live off their portfolios, bonds seem like their only choice. They need income, so they plunk for bonds, because bonds kick off more immediate income than either cash investments or stocks.

Buying investments based on yield, however, can be mighty dangerous. Indeed, many of the mutual-fund industry's biggest disasters over the past dozen years were caused by reckless fund companies offering bond funds that promised abnormally high yields with only slight risk to principal. Sure enough, government-plus funds, junk-bond funds, short-term global income funds and derivatives-stacked government bond funds delivered pumped-up dividend checks for a while. But the risks eventually caught up with these funds. Their share prices—and the dividends they paid—took a dive, badly hurting conservative investors.

Even if you pick your bonds and bond funds carefully and thus avoid such disasters, you still haven't protected principal. True, your bonds may trade around par and your fund's share price may hold up well. But if you spend your dividend checks while your portfolio's value stagnates, you are losing ground to inflation.

So what should income-hungry investors do? Fortunately, yield isn't the only way to get income from a portfolio. To generate spending money, you can also sell securities. This won't involve paying a commission or other trading costs if the money is in a no-load mutual fund. Clearly, there's the risk that your stock and bond funds will be underwater when it comes time to sell. But if you are retired and living off your savings, you can get around this problem by calculating your spending needs for the next few years and then, when the stock and bond markets seem buoyant, selling securities and moving the proceeds to a money-market fund. Indeed, as a cushion, you might keep two or three years of spending money in a money-market fund. When stocks and bonds are going through one of their periodic bloodbaths, you can tap this cash reserve for spending money, thereby avoiding the need to sell stocks and bonds at rock-bottom prices.

If you are willing to sell securities to get spending money, rather than just trying to live off your portfolio's interest and dividend payments, you are no longer compelled to buy bonds because of your desperate need for yield. Instead, you can invest for total return. If you recall, total return is a portfolio's true return. It includes not only the dividends and interest paid out by your portfolio, but also any gains or losses in the value of your portfolio's securities. So where can you get the highest total return? Stocks, of course.

Bonds, like cash, shouldn't be thought of as a stand-alone investment. Sure, if you have an investment goal coming up in the next two to five years, simply purchasing a bond or bond fund may be your best choice. But if you are investing in retirement, or saving for retirement, or socking away money for your toddler's college education, stocks should be your portfolio's engine of growth, with bonds playing only a supporting role. Viewed from that perspective, I find most bonds and bond funds unappealing. But four types of bonds can be fine additions to a stock portfolio.

Short-Term Bond Funds

These funds may be sensitive to interest rates, but they aren't nearly as sensitive as longer-term bonds. Indeed, if we get a bear market spurred by rising interest rates, short-term bond funds should provide a fairly good cushion for your stock portfolio. You might also use one of these funds as a substitute for at least part of your money-market fund holdings. Consider no-load funds such as Dreyfus Short-Intermediate Government Fund, Fidelity Short-Term Bond Portfolio, USAA Short-Term Bond Fund, Vanguard Short-Term Corporate Portfolio and Vanguard Short-Term Federal Bond Portfolio.

Short-Term Municipal-Bond Funds

Unlike most bonds, municipals don't generate hefty annual tax bills. The interest thrown off by these bonds is exempt from federal taxes. You can usually avoid state and local taxes as well, if you own bonds from your own state. But there is a tradeoff: Municipals offer lower yields than regular taxable bonds. If your income is taxed at the 28 percent marginal rate or higher, it's usually worth accepting this lower yield, because the tax saving more than compensates for the lower interest payments.

Just as you might use a short-term bond fund to cushion the stocks in your portfolio, so you can do the same with a short-term municipal bond fund. Check out funds like Dreyfus Short-Intermediate Municipal Bond Fund, Fidelity Limited-Term Municipal Income Fund, T. Rowe Price Tax-Free Short-Intermediate Fund, USAA Tax-Exempt Short-Term Fund, Vanguard Municipal Limited-Term Portfolio and Vanguard Municipal Short-Term Portfolio. If you live in a high-tax state, also look into single-state municipal bond funds, which will kick off interest that's exempt from federal, state and local taxes. The problem is, single-state funds typically own bonds with a long time to maturity, so your investment could get roughed up if interest rates rise sharply.

Zero-Coupon Bonds

With a zero, you don't receive interest every year. Instead, you buy these bonds at a discount to their final maturity value and then profit as the discount narrows. Because you don't have to worry about investing your interest payments each year, you know exactly what your return will be between now and the bond's maturity date. No other investment offers this degree of certainty. Moreover, like other Treasury bonds, zero-coupon Treasuries can't be called in early and there's no default risk.

But there are drawbacks, which deter some buyers. First, you don't receive annual interest payments, which many investors find comforting. Second, even though zeros don't pay any interest each year, you do have to pay taxes on the imputed income, so you may prefer to hold the bonds in a retirement account. Third, zeros are highly volatile. They may provide unrivaled certainty if held to maturity, but getting there can be rough.

Despite these drawbacks, I believe zeros can be a useful complement to a stock portfolio, especially for nervous investors. Imagine that you are investing your three-year-old daughter's $10,000 college fund. You want to buy stocks, but you hate the idea that the money could be devoured in a market crash. What to do? Consider the following strategy. Put enough into zero-coupon bonds to guarantee that you will have $10,000 in 15 years. Then plunk the rest of the $10,000 in stocks. If interest rates are 6.5 percent, you would have to pay around $3,900 to purchase zeros that would be worth $10,000 in 15 years. The value of that $10,000 will be somewhat diminished by 15 years of inflation and the $6,100 that you put into stocks will probably fare far better. But in the unlikely event that all your stocks become worthless, you have the comfort of knowing that you will definitely have $10,000 when your daughter reaches college age.

Adding zeros for portfolio protection may seem like an elaborate piece of self-deception. True enough. But if the deception gets you to buy stocks, it's entirely worthwhile. To purchase zeros, I would either buy individual Treasury zeros through a discount broker or one of the zero-coupon Treasury funds offered by American Century Investments, the Kansas City, Missouri, fund group formed by the merger of Twentieth Century Mutual Funds and Benham Group. Unlike most mutual funds, American Century's zero-coupon funds do actually mature, so you get the same certainty that you get with an individual bond. American Century charges for its services, of course, so you should earn higher returns by sticking with individual bonds. But the American Century funds may be a better bet, if you have a relatively small amount to invest, you plan to add to your account regularly or you think you might have to sell your bonds before they mature.

Inflation-Indexed Treasury Bonds

These bonds, which were first launched in January 1997, are a great addition to a stock portfolio. How do they work? The bonds provide a guaranteed rate of return above the inflation rate. Every year, both the bond's principal value and the amount of interest you receive gets stepped up along with inflation, as measured by the consumer price index. The interest rate itself is established by auction, when the bonds are first issued. At the inaugural auction in early 1997, the yield was 3.45 percent. This yield represents the amount you earn each year above the inflation rate. Thus, if inflation runs at 2.5 percent a year and the yield is set at 3.45 percent, your principal value will grow at 2.5 percent and every year you will receive interest equal to 3.45 percent of this ever-bigger principal value.

Despite their guarantee of inflation protection, inflation-indexed bonds aren't likely to ever match the popularity of regular Treasury bonds. The fact is, the cash yield you get with an inflation-indexed bond is relatively modest and it will change from year to year, so the bonds won't appeal to many conservative, yield-obsessed investors. Moreover, with inflation-indexed bonds, you have to pay income tax each year not only on the interest you receive, but also on the step-up in the bond's principal value. At times of high inflation and hence rapid increases in the principal value of inflation-indexed bonds, this can mean the bonds have "negative cash flow," because the cash interest you receive fails to cover your annual tax bill.

Nonetheless, inflation-indexed bonds are a great addition to a stock portfolio. Why? For owners of both conventional bonds and stocks, one of the biggest threats is rising interest rates. While interest rates fluctuate for all sorts of reasons, a key influence is inflation. When inflation picks up, interest rates rise, prompting stocks and conventional bonds to tumble. But under the same scenario, inflation-indexed bonds should prosper, as rising inflation drives up the price of—and interest paid by—these bonds.

What if stocks tumble because of a slowdown in earnings growth caused by recession? In that situation, inflation will likely slow and interest rates will drop, prompting conventional bonds to post bigger gains than inflation-indexed bonds. But inflation-indexed bonds should still hold up well, thus providing gains that partially offset your stock-market losses.

Intrigued? Consider buying individual inflation-indexed bonds, either directly from the government through the Treasury Direct program or by going through a discount broker. Alternatively, you can purchase a mutual fund that invests in these bonds. American Century offers a no-load fund that buys inflation-indexed bonds. The minimum is $2,500.

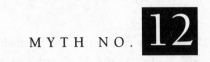

HEDGE YOUR BETS
WITH HARD ASSETS

The term "hard assets" covers a multitude of sins, everything from gold to oil to baseball cards to antiques to real estate. These are all tangible assets—they are things—as opposed to financial assets, such as stocks, bonds and cash investments, which are just pieces of paper that give the holder a narrowly defined monetary claim.

So why do you want to own hard assets? The ignorant will tell you they are a good investment. The paranoid will tell you they are the only safe investment. The sophisticated will tell you they are a good way to diversify other investments. But I'd tell you not to bother.

Every so often, particular hard assets come into vogue and they can post huge short-term price gains. Impressionist paintings soar. Baseball cards become all the rage. Gold and silver take off. That leads many to assume that these hard assets are a good investment. They are not. Over the long haul, most hard assets will generate gains that roughly match the rise in inflation. Hard assets, however, won't rise in lockstep with inflationary increases. If your timing is good and you are lucky enough to buy when baseball cards are cheap and sell when they are pricey, you could do quite nicely. But in all likelihood, your gains will match the rise in consumer prices, and that's it.

That, however, isn't a bad attribute. How so? When inflation spikes up, most stocks and bonds get roughed up. Meanwhile, hard assets can perform handsomely. Because they are recognized as a store of value—they are real assets that should maintain their value in the face of rising consumer prices—investors flock to hard assets at times of inflationary bursts or general economic and political uncertainty. Indeed, neurotic investors, who believe the end of the world is nigh, are often big holders of hard assets, particularly precious metals like gold and silver.

Those who are somewhat less skittish, however, tend to own hard assets as a way to diversify their stock-market investments. Just as bonds and cash are used to mute the risk of owning stocks, so hard assets are bought for the same reason. This is, I believe, the only legitimate investment use for hard assets. But it's still fraught with difficulties. Many hard assets are expensive to own and troublesome to trade. Most generate rotten long-run returns. And those that don't generate lousy returns tend to be lousy diversifiers for a stock portfolio.

Where We Go Wrong

Lots of folks like to collect antiques, art, baseball cards, jewelry, comic books and stamps. If you question these people, many will tell you—with a straight face, no less—that the real reason they buy these hard assets is that they are a good investment.

In one sense, they can be a good investment, because they pay fat dividends to their owners. The dividend, however, isn't of the cash variety. Rather, it is the pleasure that folks get from having fine art on their walls or antique furniture gracing their living room. But what about actual monetary gain? That, I am afraid, is likely to be a disappointment. If the value of your comic books and your antique end table matches the pace of inflation, consider yourself lucky.

Moreover, if you do try to cash in on this modest gain, you will find that selling hard assets is anything but easy. All of the potential buyers will want to inspect the item before they buy. Bids can vary enormously. Even the exact same antique end table, comic book or stamp can vary in price, depending upon the condition of the item. Because there is no central marketplace, you can't be sure whether even the highest bid is a fair one. So maybe you decide to hang on to your hard assets. This, unfortunately, also isn't cheap. If they are truly valuable, you may want to take out extra insurance or store them in a safe-deposit box. You may need to get them cleaned periodically or repaired. Such hard assets, in fact, turn out to be more of a millstone than a money-maker. You should buy baseball cards, jewelry and antiques if you like to collect them. But don't expect to get rich.

Because of the difficulties of buying, selling and holding collectibles, some—who aren't buying hard assets as collector's items—prefer to invest in commodities, such as aluminum, copper, oil and gold. With many of these hard assets, actually owning the commodity is too burdensome, so instead investors purchase futures contracts, which are paper claims that give you the right to buy a fixed quantity of the commodity at a predetermined price at a future date. These future contracts are traded on commodity exchanges, both here and abroad.

Dabbling in commodity futures is a game for big-time investors, not you and me. And the fact that institutional investors play the game doesn't mean it's a game worth playing. Returns from trading commodity futures are often horrible, the pitfalls are too numerous to list and the costs involved are astounding, especially if you invest through a commodity fund. Don't do it.

But there is one commodity that's relatively inexpensive to trade and for which you don't have to buy futures contracts, because there isn't a huge storage problem. That, of course, is gold. Indeed, for many investors, gold is synonymous with the term "hard assets." All you have to do is purchase a couple of one-ounce gold coins, such as the American Eagle, Krugerrand or Maple Leaf, pop them in a safe-deposit box that rents for maybe $30 a year and you are ready for Armageddon.

Unfortunately, if Armageddon doesn't get here soon, you may be disappointed with your returns. While year-to-year results have varied enormously, over the long haul gold—as possibly the preeminent store of value—generates returns comparable to the inflation rate. Simply matching inflation, of course, is hardly a way to build wealth. You want to do better than that? You have to look elsewhere.

Many have. Real estate is a popular choice. If you own real estate, you can garner far better returns than you would with gold. Most of the return takes the form of rent, not price appreciation, so simply buying raw land won't do it. You have to become a landlord, with all the related hassles. Buying and selling real estate is also far more involved than trading gold, as well as being far more expensive. Most experts argue—correctly, in my view—that if you own your own home, you already have plenty of real-estate exposure.

So if you are not going to buy gold, real estate and collectibles, because of low returns or high trading costs, what are you going to buy? Many have pinned their hopes on securities that promise to behave like hard assets.

You might, for instance, invest in the stocks of companies whose primary business is the production, extraction or sale of hard assets, such as gold- and silver-mining companies, oil and gas corporations, commodity producers in the copper, aluminum and timber business and real-estate investment trusts that make money by buying and then renting out real estate. These seem like hard-asset investments, yet they offer the chance to earn returns that outpace inflation. There is a good reason, however, why these investments outpace inflation. They are not hard assets. They are stocks. And because they are stocks, they tend to behave like other stocks. Result? When the broad market tumbles, these stocks often aren't spared.

The New Rules

The most effective long-term hedge against inflation isn't hard assets. It's stocks. Over the long haul, stocks are your best bet for earning healthy gains that handily beat back the twin threats of inflation and taxes. But stocks are erratic performers over the short run and will likely plunge if inflation starts to accelerate. What's the best way to hedge this short-run risk?

A lot of smart folks advocate the Noah's Ark approach to diversification. Buy two of everything in the hope of getting the broadest possible diversification. Throw in bonds, cash, stocks, hard assets, the kitchen sink. This isn't quite as foolish as it sounds. When markets become unhinged, usually one or two sectors do surprisingly well. But it's hard to predict which sectors those will be. History is a rotten guide. Markets constantly surprise. So why not toss a little gold, maybe a few real-estate investment trusts and a couple of timber companies into the mix, in the hope that, when everything else becomes unglued, at least one of these will stick?

I think this is a messy, unreliable way to build a portfolio, especially when we have two financial assets that are almost certain to provide ballast for a portfolio at times of market turmoil. Which two assets? Cash investments and inflation-indexed bonds.

Though we don't have a lot of experience with inflation-indexed Treasury bonds, the structure of these bonds makes them a fine choice for those looking to diversify a portfolio of financial assets, and particularly stocks. Inflation-indexed bonds should hold their own in recession. Meanwhile, like hard assets, these bonds will rise in value along with increases in consumer prices. In fact, you are guaranteed to outpace inflation with inflation-indexed bonds. Hard assets, by contrast, come with no such guarantee and the short-run performance can be entirely fickle.

As I mentioned earlier, if you purchase inflation-indexed bonds, the principal value of your bonds is stepped up each year, along with the consumer price index. If inflation runs at 3 percent a year between now and the bond's maturity date, the value of your inflation-indexed bonds will get boosted at this rate. The interest payments kicked off by the bonds will also rise along with inflation. If the interest rate on the bonds is 3.5 percent, every year you will receive interest equal to 3.5 percent of the bond's growing principal value.

Cash investments, such as Treasury bills, commercial paper and money-market funds, also offer a fine way to fend off short-term inflationary bursts. By definition, these investments mature within less than a year. Money-market funds, for instance, are required by law to own debt instruments that, on average, have less than 90 days to maturity. With a money-market fund, you shouldn't ever find yourself locked into a lousy yield relative to inflation, because you are never locking in a yield. Your money-market fund's Treasury bills and commercial paper will mature constantly and get replaced by new securities. The yield on these new securities will reflect prevailing concerns about inflation (or the lack thereof), so that your money-market fund earns returns close to or somewhat ahead of inflation. This isn't the stuff that fortunes are made of. But it does provide dependable ballast for a stock portfolio, which great fortunes are made of.

Cash and inflation-indexed bonds won't give you the sort of explosive, eye-popping returns that you might get with hard assets, especially gold. When inflation heats up and most stocks and bonds get decimated, gold can soar, providing the sort of exaggerated gains that can help a sagging portfolio. The problem is, these gains aren't reliable. By contrast, you can be confident that cash and inflation-indexed bonds—while they won't go through the roof—will post decent results during an inflationary spurt. They offer what you want from hard assets, but don't get—reliable portfolio protection.

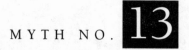

YOU SHOULD OWN A BALANCED PORTFOLIO

Here—in its unabridged version—is Wall Street's formula for financial happiness. It doesn't involve any fancy strategies or bizarre investments. You don't need to guess the market's direction, or buy pork belly futures, or sell stocks short, or invest in naked puts.

Instead, you take your investment portfolio and divide it, putting 60 percent into stocks and 40 percent into bonds. Usually, the stock portion goes into blue-chip companies, while the bond portion is given over to a mix of longer-term government and corporate bonds. Thereafter, you save regularly and, every so often, make sure that you are still holding stocks and bonds in the right proportions. The stocks will give you growth, the bonds will give you income. When stocks are struggling, the bonds will take up the slack, and vice versa. Folks have been investing this way for generations, and the strategy is still widely followed today by investors large and small.

It's a swell idea. It's just a damn shame it doesn't work.

Where We Go Wrong

What's wrong with the traditional balanced portfolio? The mix of 60 percent stocks and 40 percent bonds is unnecessarily volatile and, for many investors, it's way too conservative. Gone are the days when stocks and bonds moved independently, so that bonds might rally when stocks are plunging. Since the 1970s, these two assets have moved increasingly in lockstep, as stocks have become more sensitive to interest rates, just like bonds. Result? When bonds dive, stocks usually follow. Balanced portfolios, it seems, just don't live up to their name.

This is bad news for a lot of investors, but especially for retirees. If you are recently retired, a balanced portfolio would seem to make a lot of sense. After all, you could easily live another 25 years, which is plenty of time to enjoy the superior long-run returns that stocks can generate. In fact, with folks living longer in retirement, investing in stocks isn't just possible, it's necessary. If you don't get some decent growth from your portfolio, your standard of living will be ravaged by inflation.

But if you are retired, you also need to tap your investments every year for income, and the dividends and interest from your balanced portfolio probably won't be enough to cover your spending needs. So you may need to sell securities every year. What happens if the stocks and bonds in your balanced portfolio sink simultaneously? You could end up selling securities at depressed prices.

Balanced portfolios also aren't a good bet for those saving for retirement. Unless you are close to quitting the work force, a mix of 60 percent stocks and 40 percent bonds seems far too conservative. Why do you need all those bonds? Sure, they generate a fair amount of income. But you don't need income. You still have a salary. Yeah, the bonds will help to calm your stock portfolio. But they don't help very much. Own a balanced portfolio? The whole thing just doesn't make any sense.

The New Rules

What does make sense? You want to maintain the goal of the traditional balanced portfolio, which is to invest in stocks while adding investments that will reduce risk and—if you are retired—make it possible to tap your portfolio for income. How do you manage that? Here are three suggestions.

Stocks and Zero-Coupon Bonds

Zero-coupon bonds are, if anything, more volatile than stocks. Because these bonds don't pay any interest each year, they respond wildly to interest-rate changes. But if you hold them to maturity, you know exactly what you will earn with a zero-coupon bond. You buy the bonds at a discount to their final maturity value and then profit as the discount narrows. You don't even have to worry about reinvesting your interest payments, because there are no payments to reinvest.

Zeros can be a great comfort to nervous investors, just so long as you can focus on the bond's final maturity value and ignore all the wild price swings along the way. Suppose you are 20 years from retirement. You don't mind putting some of your money in stocks. But you want to be confident that, when you finally quit the work force, you have 25 percent of your portfolio sitting in cash. This cash will provide the spending money that carries you through your initial retirement years.

How do you generate this cash cushion, while still getting healthy investment gains? Take some money and purchase zero-coupon bonds that mature close to your expected retirement date. Alternatively, you might buy one of American Century Investments' zero-coupon bond funds, which mature at five-year intervals. If you are buying 20-year zeros and interest rates are around 6.5 percent, you will have to hand over 28 cents today to get bonds that are worth one dollar in 20 years.

Let's say you figure you will have a $1-million portfolio at retirement, which means you would want to own zeros that will mature 20 years from now and, at that point, be worth $250,000.

To guarantee that $250,000, you could simply shovel some $71,000 into zeros today and then, over the final 20 years of your retirement, stash every last penny into stocks. While that's not a bad strategy, I would be inclined to put most of your portfolio into stocks today and then gradually buy zeros that will mature in the year you retire. By doing it this way, you would have more of your money in stocks today, which should translate into higher returns. In addition, you avoid committing a big chunk to zeros all at once, which would lock in a yield and leave you vulnerable to inflation.

The stock-zeros mix allows you to commit a hefty chunk of your portfolio to stocks and get fairly good returns from your bonds, while at the same time guaranteeing that you will have a pool of cash ready to spend when you reach retirement. The portfolio's weakness is its volatility. If you can't focus on the final maturity value of the zeros and instead fixate on the day-to-day price swings, you could find it unnerving to own the stock-zeros mix. But for those who can look beyond the daily price gyrations, I think the 75 percent stocks–25 percent zeros combination is better than a traditional balanced portfolio, with its mix of 60 percent stocks and 40 percent bonds, and it should generate superior returns.

Stocks and Inflation-Indexed Bonds

Instead of buying stocks and zeros, you could mix stocks and inflation-indexed bonds. You can't lock in a return with inflation-indexed bonds, as you can with zeros, and inflation-indexed bonds will likely lag behind zeros and conventional bonds during periods of falling interest rates. But inflation-indexed bonds are in many ways a better complement to stocks. When inflation accelerates, stocks, conventional bonds and zeros get bludgeoned. But inflation-indexed bonds will climb. You also know that your inflation-indexed bonds, unlike zeros and other more conventional bonds, won't get ravaged by a protracted rise in consumer prices.

You could use a mix of inflation-indexed bonds and stocks both when saving for retirement and when investing in retire-

Too Close for Comfort

Owning stocks is nerve-wracking. Selling can be even worse.

As you get closer to your financial goals, you need to yank money out of stocks and plunk it into more conservative investments. But when do you make the shift? Here's a look at how to handle your money when dealing with three of the most costly financial goals.

■ If you are saving to buy a house, you should start shifting the money out of stocks and into a short-term bond fund when you are five years from making your home purchase. Once you are within 18 months of buying a house, swap the money into a money-market fund.

Why start selling stocks five years from when you will need the money? While stocks should earn handsome gains over that stretch, there have been some five-year spells during which stocks have lost money. If you can take a market hit and still afford your dream house or if you could borrow money to cover any shortfall, you might risk leaving some of the money in stocks over this final stretch. But if any loss would devastate your chances of buying a home, start swapping your savings out of stocks five years ahead of time, preferably making your stock sales when the market is buoyant.

■ While you need to pony up thousands of dollars on a single day when you buy a house, paying for college is more drawn out. If you are going to put, say, a quarter of young Harold's college savings toward paying for his freshman year, you might pull this money out of stocks five years before he starts college. Similarly, you might pull another quarter of his savings out of stocks five years before his sophomore year. Ditto for the money earmarked for the junior and senior years.

Seem too conservative? You could leave the money in stocks for longer knowing that, if the market tanks, you will cover college costs by borrowing money or dipping into other savings, while you wait for stocks to bounce back. But before adopting this strategy, make sure you have the temperament to see it through.

■ Your retirement savings might have to last 25 years. As a result, even after you quit the work force, you still need growth from your investments and that means owning stocks. Indeed, I believe retirees should keep at least half their money in stocks. What about tapping your portfolio for spending money? As you near retirement, gradually shift some money out of stocks and into more conservative investments. By the time you retire, aim to have 25 percent of your portfolio in a money-market fund and short-term bonds. This money will cover your spending needs for the first four years or so of retirement, while the rest of your portfolio continues to generate the investment growth needed to ensure that your retirement lifestyle isn't ravaged by inflation.

ment. Until you retire, the only role for the inflation-indexed bonds is to lower your portfolio's risk level. The more you have in bonds, the lower your long-run returns, so put enough in inflation-indexed bonds to let you sleep at night and then shovel the rest into stocks. Unless you are within 10 years of retirement, I wouldn't put more than 20 percent of your portfolio into bonds.

As you approach retirement, or once you are retired, you should move up to 40 percent of your portfolio into inflation-indexed bonds. With a mix of 60 percent stocks and 40 percent bonds, you should be able to withdraw about 6 percent of your portfolio's value each year and still get enough growth so that you can step up your annual withdrawals along with inflation. This 6 percent includes the dividends and interest payments you receive. Indeed, each year, look to spend all the interest generated by your bonds and all the dividends kicked off by your stocks. If you own mutual funds, you can also spend the capital-gains distributions you receive. After tapping these sources of income, you should—if necessary—sell stocks and bonds to hit your 6 percent withdrawal target. If stocks are booming, unload some of these. But if the stock market is in a funk, tap the bond side of your portfolio.

Stocks and Cash Investments

If you are retired, instead of owning stocks and inflation-indexed bonds, you could combine stocks and cash investments,

The 6 Percent Solution

How much income will your savings generate once you retire? As a starting point, bank on withdrawing 6 percent of your portfolio's value in the first year of retirement. Thereafter, increase your annual withdrawals along with inflation.

For instance, if you retire with $500,000, you would withdraw $30,000 in the first year of retirement. If inflation runs at 3 percent a year, boost your annual withdrawal by 3 percent to $30,900 in year two, $31,827 in year three, and so on. These withdrawals include any dividends, interest and mutual-fund distributions kicked off by your portfolio. Not all of the money withdrawn can be spent, however. After all, even after you retire, you still have to pay taxes.

Here's the reasoning behind the 6 percent figure. Suppose you own a portfolio of 60 percent stocks and 40 percent bonds or a mix of 75 percent stocks and 25 percent cash investments. If inflation runs at 3 percent a year, stocks would likely deliver around 10 percent annually, bonds might return 6.5 percent and cash investments could earn 4.5 percent. After making allowances for investment costs, your portfolio might gain somewhat less than 8 percent a year. Thus, with a 6 percent withdrawal rate, you would—during the initial years of retirement—be leaving a small part of each year's investment gains in the portfolio, so that your portfolio might grow at maybe 1 percent or 1.5 percent a year, somewhat less than inflation.

Why can't you spend each year's entire investment gains? If you did that, your portfolio's principal value would be quickly eroded by inflation, thus crimping your lifestyle later in retirement. At 3 percent inflation, the value of your portfolio—and the investment earnings it generates—would be cut in half after 23 years. That's a real danger for today's retirees. If you quit the work force at age 65, the mortality tables suggest you will live until age 85. But remember that 85 is merely an average. Half of all those who are currently 65 will live beyond age 85. If you retire at 65 and you are in good health, you should really plan as though you will live until at least age 90. Your retirement could last 25 years or more.

Does a 6 percent withdrawal rate seem like too little? It may well be. But because you don't know when you will die, you can't plan your finances so that you run out of money when you run out of breath. Like it or not, you will almost inevitably leave some money to your ungrateful and undeserving heirs.

If a 6 percent withdrawal isn't enough to sustain the sort of retirement lifestyle you want, you could delay retirement for a few years. While a 6 percent withdrawal rate is reasonable if you retire at 65 and face a potential 25-year retirement, you might opt for a 7 percent or higher withdrawal rate if you delay retirement to age 70. By that point, your retirement kitty should also be somewhat larger, because you will have had more time to save and your money will have had more time to grow.

Alternatively, you could retire at 65 and gamble on a withdrawal rate higher than 6 percent, either because your family health history or your own medical condition suggests that you have a shorter life expectancy or because you are willing to spend more early in retirement, knowing that you will cut back later if you have to. Indeed, many retirees spend more in the early years of retirement, when they travel and go out more, and less once they get to 80 and beyond.

What if you retire at age 60 or earlier? You could be 30 or more years in retirement, so you should stick with a 5 percent withdrawal rate. Why only 5 percent? Every year, you need to plow a hefty chunk of your annual investment earnings back into your portfolio, so that your portfolio's value continues to grow almost as fast as inflation.

such as a money-market fund or Treasury bills. Cash investments will generate lower returns than inflation-indexed bonds, so instead of combining 60 percent stocks and 40 percent bonds, you might mix 75 percent stocks and 25 percent cash. In his November 15, 1988, economic commentary, Peter L. Bernstein, a New York economic consultant and author of *Capital Ideas: The Improbable Origins of Modern Wall Street* (Free Press, 1992) and *Against the Gods: The Remarkable Story of Risk* (John Wiley & Sons, 1996), noted that a mix of 75 percent stocks and 25 percent cash was no more risky than a traditional balanced portfolio with 60 percent stocks and 40 percent conventional bonds. The stock-cash mix, however, had slightly better returns.

While a mix of 75 percent stocks and 25 percent cash may be superior to 60 percent stocks and 40 percent conventional bonds, it's not clear that the stock-cash combo is better than a mix of 60 percent stocks and 40 percent inflation-indexed bonds. But the stock-cash combination is still an appealing option. For those who find investing nerve-wracking, the stock-cash mix offers an enormous amount of comfort. It's conceivable, for instance, that both stocks and inflation-indexed bonds might tumble at the same time, because interest rates rise without a corresponding rise in inflation. But with the stock-cash mix, you know your cash is never going to drop in value.

This makes it easy to tap your portfolio for spending money. With 25 percent of your portfolio in cash, you are sitting with a cushion equal to over four years of annual income, presuming you aim to withdraw 6 percent of your portfolio's value each year. If your cash investments are sitting in a money-market fund, getting spending money is as simple as writing a check. Because money-market funds seek to maintain a stable one-dollar share price, you shouldn't ever have a capital gain or loss when writing checks, so there won't be any messy tax accounting. Every year, look to sell some stocks and move the proceeds to your money-market fund, to replenish the cash you withdrew from there. What if stocks fall out of bed? Don't sell until the stock market recovers. With 25 percent of your portfolio in a money-market fund, you can sit tight for more than four years without selling any stocks.

Is that long enough? As I noted earlier, since World War II, there have been a couple of five-year stretches when stocks have lost money. Those losing streaks occurred because there were two market drops within five years, one at the beginning of the period and one at the end. No bear market since World War II has actually lasted five years. How bad has it gotten? The worst postwar bear market was the 1973–74 market crash. From the market peak at year-end 1972, it took 3½ years to get back to even, as measured by the total return of the Standard & Poor's 500-stock index. With over four years of spending money in a money-market fund, you could have weathered even that ferocious bear market.

If you want to take a little more risk with some of your cash investments, you could put part of the money in a short-term taxable bond fund or a short-term municipal-bond fund. This would introduce a few more hassles into managing your portfolio, but should boost your returns. You could also mix and match some of the elements from each of the three portfolios above. Those saving for retirement might split their bond investments between zeros and inflation-indexed bonds. Those who are retired might combine inflation-indexed bonds, short-term bond funds and money-market funds. Similarly, for the stock portion of the portfolio, you could invest in both actively managed stock funds and index funds, or you might just plunk for index funds. There is no right answer. A lot depends on your temperament, how much hassle you are willing to endure and what investments make you most comfortable.

But whatever you do, remember what's important. Adding bonds and cash simply reduces your stock portfolio's risk level and makes it easy to tap your portfolio for income. Investing in actively managed stock funds is more likely to get you market-lagging returns than market-beating results. The key to good returns is to keep as much money as possible in stocks, while ensuring that you are broadly diversified and that you minimize investment costs, so that you get returns that approach the market averages. That strategy—combined with time, patience and a commitment to save regularly—should provide you with ample riches.

MYTH NO.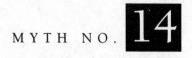

YOU NEED A BROKER

Your parents needed a broker. You don't.

Broker bashing? Not at all. I just want you to understand that you have a choice. I am constantly amazed by the number of novice investors I meet who believe they can't actually buy or sell an investment without going through a broker. It just isn't so.

Wall Street has changed radically since the mid-1970s. The business of giving investment advice has become much more competitive, thanks to the emergence of thousands of financial planners. These planners, who don't just peddle investments but instead aim to provide investors with comprehensive financial plans, now offer a credible alternative to brokers. And if you don't want to pay for advice, you can bypass planners and brokers entirely, thereby saving yourself a small fortune. Before the 1970s, virtually all mutual funds levied a sales commission when you bought or sold. Today, a huge number of funds are offered without a load.

Brokerage commissions to trade individual stocks have also plummeted over the past two decades. Full-service brokerage firms like Merrill Lynch & Co. and Smith Barney are now challenged by discount brokers, who eschew giving advice and instead merely complete transactions. For their pains, discount brokers charge just a fraction of the commission levied by their full-service competitors. But even discount brokers are starting to look pricey. Investors can now buy shares directly from a burgeoning number of publicly traded companies, with little or nothing charged in fees and commissions.

Yet with all this change, many investors still automatically plunk for a full-service broker. This may turn out to be their best choice. But it sure isn't the only one.

Where We Go Wrong

There are right and wrong reasons for employing a full-service broker. The wrong reasons? A lot of folks use brokers because they think they will get market-beating results or because they believe investing is just too complicated to do on their own. The brokerage industry, of course, hasn't done a whole lot to dispel these two myths. But the truth is, brokers are trained primarily to be good salesmen, not good investment advisers.

Using a broker could still improve your investment results, however, especially if the broker can persuade you to put more money into stocks and then get you to stick with these investments through the inevitable market turmoil. But don't expect market-beating returns. Just as most money managers don't outpace the market averages, so brokers also fail. Consider, for instance, broker-sold stock funds. Thanks to rising expenses, these funds tend to lag not only the market, but also their no-load fund competitors.

What about all the complexity of investing? On that score, brokers sometimes compare themselves to lawyers or accountants or even doctors. The analogy doesn't work. If you need a will drawn up, or you have a complicated tax question, or you are about to drop dead from some nasty disease, you might try to tackle the problem yourself. But even if you are smart and diligent, you could still mess up royally. And if you do get it wrong, the consequences may prove dire. Unfortunately, in these instances, there's really no substitute for going to a lawyer or an accountant or a doctor.

With many of our financial dealings, however, we turn to professionals because it's the easiest way to go. You could sell your home on your own, but it's a lot simpler to go through a real-estate broker. You could save money by shopping around for life insurance, but you use an agent because it's more convenient. You could do your own taxes, but it's much quicker to turn over all those 1099s and W-2s to a tax preparer.

The same is true for investing. It isn't that complicated. Sure, there's a lot of confusing rubbish, like options, futures, mortgage derivatives and limited partnerships, which you would be well-advised to ignore. But at its core, investing is about the issues discussed in this book. Rocket science, it isn't.

So why bother with a broker? Two reasons: hand-holding and convenience. Hand-holding is the most overlooked reason for using a broker, but also the most important. The toughest part of investing isn't figuring out what you should do with your money. Instead, the toughest part, I believe, is getting yourself to do what you know is right. Investing is fraught with psychological pitfalls and some folks just can't avoid them.

Investors, unfortunately, often torpedo their own financial future by trading too much, by panicking at the slightest market dip, by not saving enough, by procrastinating over investment decisions and by not shoveling enough money into stocks. Books, newspapers and personal-finance magazines may give you a very good idea of what you should do with your money. But if you can't get it done on your own, your best bet is to get an investment adviser, whether it's a broker or somebody else. The cost involved will clearly cut into your returns. But you will be better off over the long haul.

The second reason to use a broker is convenience. You might employ a broker for the same reason you hire a tax preparer, use a lawn service or pay somebody to paint the house. These are all things you could do yourself. But many of us have limited time and sometimes we find it's worth paying somebody to do these tasks for us.

But getting your money managed, whether for the hand-holding or for the convenience, is a little different from getting your lawn cut. If some local kid cuts your grass too short and the lawn turns brown, your yard may be ruined, which is unfortunate though fixable. But if your broker messes up, your financial future could be ruined, which is a little more problematic. Unless you are careful, your retirement nest egg and your kid's college savings could disappear in a string of ill-considered investments and foolish trades. You can't just hand over your money to a broker and then forget all about it. Even if your broker is entirely competent, there's no way he or she can make good investment choices without your active participation. Your broker has to know what your goals are, what investments you are comfortable with and what changes are occurring that affect your finances. You have to stay involved.

You also have to stay vigilant. It's not that brokers are crooks. The vast majority aren't. But the relationship between broker and client isn't always mutually beneficial. Traditionally, brokers have received much of their compensation from commissions, which means they make money when you do something. If you don't buy and sell, they don't get paid. If your broker is unscrupulous, he or she will push you to make unnecessary trades. At the extreme, you get cases of churning, in which a broker—with or without the client's consent—trades the account like a dervish, generating heaps of commission dollars for the broker and horrible investment returns for the client.

Fortunately, commission-based compensation for brokers is on the wane. Prodded by competition from financial planners, who get compensated largely or entirely through fees rather than commissions, many big brokerage houses are introducing their own fee-based programs. Rather than paying a commission every time you trade, brokerage firms will now charge an annual fee for putting you into no-load mutual funds or levy a yearly fee that covers a set number of stock trades. The annual fee might be, say, 1.5 percent of the assets you have with the broker.

These fee arrangements remove the conflict of interest that brokers have. But it still leaves a more basic problem: It's a lot of money. Moreover, if your portfolio is worth less than $50,000, you may find it hard to persuade a broker or financial planner to manage your money for a fee and, even if you do find somebody, the annual charge could be even steeper than 1.5 percent. Your returns will inevitably suffer. Are you sure it's worth the price?

The New Rules

Is it worth paying a broker or financial planner to manage your money? For most investors, I believe the answer is a resounding no. Ignore all the self-interested experts telling you that you need a professional's help. Investing isn't that complicated and you could probably do just fine on your own. It's not merely a matter of saving money and thus boosting your returns. Indeed, if you go it alone, your returns may actually suffer in the early years, as you learn how to invest and make foolish mistakes along the way.

Eventually, however, you will get your reward, which will be measured not only in money, but also in a true sense of independence and control over your financial situation. Too many folks are dominated by their finances, by the litany of debts and the gnawing feeling that maybe they aren't saving enough and maybe they aren't doing the right things. If you make the effort to understand your finances and understand investing, you can overcome these doubts and achieve some genuine financial freedom.

And yes, you will save yourself a bundle. For the penny-pinching do-it-yourselfer, there are three key sources of low-cost investments. First, and most important, there are no-load mutual funds. These should form at least the core of your portfolio, and there's no reason funds shouldn't be your only investment. Pay attention not only to avoiding loads, but also to holding down your annual investment costs by buying funds with low expenses.

Trading on the Cheap

Below are some of the better-known discount brokers. Web addresses are shown only if the firm offers Internet trading.

BROKERAGE FIRM	PHONE NUMBER	INTERNET ADDRESS
Accutrade	800-228-3011	www.accutrade.com
American Express Direct	800-658-4677	americanexpress.com/ direct
K. Aufhauser & Co.	800-368-3668	www.aufhauser.com
Bidwell & Co.	800-547-6337	
Brown & Co.	800-822-2021	
Ceres Securities	800-669-3900	www.ceres.com
Datek	888-463-2835	www.datek.com
Discover Brokerage	800-566-2273	lombard.com
eBroker	800-553-9513	www.ebroker.com
E*Trade	800-786-2575	www.etrade.com
Fidelity Brokerage	800-544-8666	personal.fidelity.com
R.J. Forbes Group	800-488-0090	
Kennedy, Cabot & Co.	800-252-0090	
Marquette de Bary Co.	800-221-3305	debary.com
National Discount Brokers	800-888-3999	www.ndb.com
Net Investor	800-638-4250	www.netinvestor.com
Olde Discount	800-872-6533	
Pacific Brokerage	800-421-8395	tradepbs.com
PC Financial Network	800-825-5723	www.pcfn.com
T. Rowe Price Brokerage	800-225-7720	
Quick & Reilly	800-221-5220	www.quick-reilly.com
Charles Schwab Corp.	800-435-4000	www.eschwab.com
Scottsdale Securities	800-888-1980	discountbroker.com
Seaport Securities	800-732-7678	
Muriel Siebert & Co.	800-872-0711	
StockCross	800-225-6196	
USAA Brokerage Services	800-531-8343	
Vanguard Group	800-992-8327	(continued)

Brokerage Firm	Phone Number	Internet Address
Waterhouse Securities	800-934-4430	www.waterhouse.com
Jack White & Co.	800-233-3411	www.jackwhiteco.com
York Securities	800-221-3154	

Second, if you are looking to invest in individual securities or you want to use one of the mutual-fund supermarkets that offer stock and bond funds from a host of fund families, find yourself a good discount broker. The biggest discount-brokerage firms include Charles Schwab Corporation and Fidelity Brokerage Services. Both firms offer mutual-fund supermarkets with an impressive array of funds, many of which can be bought without any sort of transaction fee. But if the only reason you want a discount broker is to trade individual securities, you can shave your costs even further by using one of the "deep discounters," which might charge less than $30 for an individual stock trade. To do a little price shopping, just glance through a copy of *Barron's*, *The Wall Street Journal* or one of the personal-finance magazines. You will likely find advertisements from at least some of the deep discounters. Alternatively, try one of the Internet discount brokers, where commissions are sometimes less than $15 a trade.

Finally, consider so-called no-load stocks. For years, investors have been able to buy mutual funds without a broker. Now, you don't even need a broker to buy individual stocks, thanks to the introduction of these no-load stock programs, which are now offered by some 300 firms, including Exxon, Gillette, Mattel, Merck and Mobil. With no-load stocks, you typically need between $50 and $1,000 to make your initial share purchase. These shares are then held in a dividend reinvestment plan, so that your dividends automatically buy additional shares. With a dividend reinvestment plan, you also can send in optional cash payments every week or every month, so that your account grows even faster.

For those who want to include individual stocks in their portfolio, no-load stocks provide a disciplined, low-cost way to build a portfolio. But don't go overboard. Keep the number of stocks you buy manageable, so that the paperwork doesn't become excessive. At the same time, make sure that you don't end up with more than 5 percent of your total stock portfolio in any one company. Some no-load stock programs are almost completely free, but others charge modest fees and commissions. Check the fine print to make sure that these costs aren't too burdensome. With those programs that charge fees when you buy shares, you may find that your best bet is to make less frequent but larger share purchases. Meanwhile, if there's an annual account fee, aim to build up your account quickly, so that the fee is spread over a bigger dollar amount and thus the percentage hit isn't so great.

You may want to sign up for a company's dividend reinvestment plan, but find that the company isn't a no-load stock and thus you can't get into the plan unless you have at least one share. What to do? In these cases, consider buying a single share through a discount broker, so that you minimize your commission costs. Alternatively, contact the National Association of Investors Corporation (810-583-6242). NAIC will help you buy a single share of some 160 different companies and then use the share to get you enrolled in the company's dividend reinvestment plan. For this service, NAIC charges an annual membership fee, as well as a small fee for each stock bought. Internet users can find a complete list of the 160 participating companies at NAIC's home page (http://better-investing.org). A similar—though somewhat more expensive—service is offered by Temper of the Times Communications (800-295-2550). Temper helps members buy a single share and then become enrolled in the dividend reinvestment plans of over 900 companies.

What if, after a few years of handling your own finances, you want to make sure you are on track? Consider contacting a broker or financial planner and asking him or her to review your finances. Call only brokers and planners who come recommended by friends, family or colleagues. Alternatively, phone the Institute of Certified Financial Planners (800-282-7526) or the National Association of Personal Financial Advisors (888-333-6659) and

Cutting Out the Middleman

The companies below will all sell shares directly to investors, with little or nothing charged in fees or commissions. Because the number of no-load stocks is exploding, keep an eye out for new plans. Information on many no-load stocks is available through the Direct Stock Purchase Plan Clearinghouse (800-774-4117). First Chicago (800-446-2617 or 800-808-2233) and Harris Trust (800-286-9178) also operate clearinghouses. A slew of foreign companies, which trade in the United States as American depositary receipts, are offered as no-load stocks through Bank of New York (800-345-1612) and J.P. Morgan (800-749-1687). Meanwhile, if you are an Internet user, check out NetStock Direct (http://netstockdirect.com), which posts an up-to-date list of all no-load stocks, and DRIP Investor (http://dripinvestor.com), a site devoted to dividend reinvestment plans.

U.S. Stocks

ABT Building Products	800-774-4117/800-286-9178
Advanta	800-774-4117/800-225-5923
Aflac	800-227-4756
AGL Resources	800-774-4117/800-866-1543
Air Products and Chemicals	888-694-9458
AirTouch Communications	800-233-5601
Ameritech	800-774-4117/888-752-6248
Amoco	800-774-4117/800-821-8100
Arrow Financial	518-745-1000
Atlantic Energy	609-645-4506
Atmos Energy	800-774-4117/800-382-8667
Bard (C.R.)	800-828-1639
Bell Atlantic	800-631-2355
BellSouth	888-266-6778
Bob Evans Farms	800-272-7675
Boston Beer Co.	888-266-6780
BRE Properties	800-774-4117/800-437-9050
Capstead Mortgage	800-969-6715
Carpenter Technology	800-822-9828

U.S. STOCKS

Central & South West	800-774-4117/800-527-5797
Central Hudson Gas & Electric	888-280-3848
Chevron	800-774-4117/800-286-9178
Chock Full O'Nuts	888-200-3161
Cilcorp	800-774-4117/800-654-1685
CMS Energy	800-774-4117/517-788-1868
Coastal	800-788-2500
Comsat	301-214-3200
Crown American Realty	800-774-4117/800-278-4353
Curtiss-Wright	888-266-6793
Dayton Hudson	888-268-0203
Dominion Resources	800-552-4034
DTE Energy	800-774-4117/800-551-5009
Duke Realty	800-774-4117/800-937-5449
Eastern Co.	800-633-3455
Emcee Broadcast Products	888-200-3167
Energen	800-774-4117/800-286-9178
Enova	800-307-7343
Enron	800-662-7662
Entergy	800-225-1721
Equifax	800-568-3476
Equitable	800-774-4117/800-923-6782
Exxon	800-252-1800
Fed One Bancorp	800-742-7540
First Commercial	800-482-8410
Food Lion	888-232-9530
Ford Motor	800-955-4791
General Growth Properties	800-774-4117/888-291-3713
Gillette	800-643-6989
Guidant	800-537-1677
Harveys Casino Resorts	888-200-3164
Hawaiian Electric Industries	808-543-5662
Hillenbrand Industries	800-774-4117/800-286-9178
Home Depot	800-774-4117/800-928-0380
Home Properties	800-774-4117/800-278-4353
Houston Industries	800-774-4117/800-231-6406

U.S. STOCKS

IBM	888-421-8860
Illinova	800-750-7011
Integon	800-826-3978
Interchange Financial Services	201-703-2265
Investors Financial	888-333-5336
Ipalco Enterprises	800-774-4117/888-847-2526
Johnson Controls	800-524-6220
Kellwood	314-576-3100
Kerr-McGee	800-395-2662
Liberty Property Trust	800-944-2214
Lucent Technologies	888-582-3686
Madison Gas & Electric	800-356-6423
Mattel	888-909-9922
McDonald's	800-774-4117/800-228-9623
Merck	800-774-4117/800-831-8248
MidAmerican Energy	800-247-5211
Minnesota Power & Light	800-774-4117/800-535-3056
Mobil	800-648-9291
Morgan Stanley, Dean Witter, Discover	800-228-0829
Morton International	800-774-4117/800-990-1010
Newport News Shipbuilding	800-649-1861
Norwest	800-774-4117/800-813-3324
OGE Energy	800-774-4117/800-395-2662
Oneok	800-395-2662
Owens Corning	800-472-2210
J.C. Penney	800-565-2576
Peoples Energy	800-774-4117/800-901-8878
Pharmacia & Upjohn	800-774-4117/800-286-9178
Philadelphia Suburban	800-774-4117/800-205-8314
Piedmont Natural Gas	800-774-4117/800-693-9917
Pinnacle West	800-774-4117/602-379-2500
Procter & Gamble	800-764-7483
Public Service Enterprise	800-242-0813
Public Service of New Mexico	800-545-4425
Public Service of North Carolina	800-774-4117/800-736-2163
Questar	800-729-6788

U.S. STOCKS

Reader's Digest	800-242-4653
Regions Financial	800-922-3468
Scana Corp.	800-763-5891
Sears, Roebuck	888-732-7788
Semco Energy	800-649-1856
Sierra Pacific Resources	800-662-7575
Sonoma Valley Bank	888-200-3163
Southern Co.	800-774-4117/800-554-7626
Southern Union	800-793-8938
Stone Container	800-346-9979
Sunstone Hotel Investors	800-774-4117/800-922-9542
Taubman Centers	800-774-4117/800-437-1329
Tenneco	800-446-2617
Texaco	800-283-9785
TNP Enterprises	800-774-4117/800-649-0629
Tribune Co.	800-924-1490
Tyson Foods	800-822-7096
U S West Communications	800-537-0222
Urban Shopping Centers	800-774-4117/800-992-4566
UtiliCorp United	800-647-2789
Viad	800-453-2235
Wal-Mart Stores	800-438-6278
Warner-Lambert	888-767-7166
Weingarten Realty Investors	888-887-2966
Western Resources	800-774-4117/800-527-2495
Whitman	800-660-4187
Wisconsin Energy	800-558-9663
WLR Foods	540-896-7001
WPS Resources	800-236-1551
Xxsys Technologies	888-200-3166
York International	800-774-4117/800-437-6726

FOREIGN STOCKS

Adecco	800-774-4117/800-749-1687
Aktiebolaget Electrolux	800-774-4117/800-749-1687
Akzo Nobel	800-774-4117/800-749-1687
Amcor Limited	800-774-4117/800-749-1687
Amway Japan	800-774-4117/800-749-1687
Asia Satellite Telecommunications	800-774-4117/800-749-1687
Banco de Santander	800-774-4117/800-749-1687
Banco Wiese	800-774-4117/800-749-1687
Bank of Tokyo-Mitsubishi	800-774-4117/800-345-1612
Barclays Bank	800-774-4117/800-749-1687
Benetton Group	800-774-4117/800-749-1687
Biora AB	800-774-4117/800-345-1612
BOC Group	800-774-4117/800-749-1687
British Airways	800-774-4117/800-749-1687
British Petroleum	800-774-4117/800-749-1687
British Telecommunications	800-774-4117/800-749-1687
Cadbury Schweppes	800-774-4117/800-749-1687
Compania Cervecerias Unidas	800-774-4117/800-749-1687
Consorcio G Grupo Dina	800-774-4117/800-749-1687
Corporacion Bancaria de España, Argentaria	800-774-4117/800-749-1687
CSR Limited	800-774-4117/800-749-1687
Dassault Systemes	800-774-4117/800-749-1687
Empresa Nacional de Electricidad	800-774-4117/800-749-1687
Fiat	800-774-4117/800-749-1687
Flamel Technologies	800-774-4117/800-345-1612
Fresenius Medical Care	800-774-4117/800-749-1687
Groupe AB	800-774-4117/800-345-1612
Grupo Casa Autrey	800-774-4117/800-749-1687
Guangshen Railway Co.	800-774-4117/800-749-1687
Huntingdon Life Sciences	800-774-4117/800-345-1612
Imperial Chemical Industries	800-774-4117/800-749-1687
Industrie Natuzzi	800-774-4117/800-345-1612
Invesco	800-774-4117/800-749-1687
Istituto Mobiliare Italiano	800-774-4117/800-749-1687
Koninklijke Ahold	800-774-4117/800-749-1687
Lihir Gold	800-774-4117/800-345-1612

FOREIGN STOCKS

London International	800-774-4117/800-345-1612
Luxottica Group	800-774-4117/800-345-1612
Makita	800-774-4117/800-345-1612
National Westminster Bank	800-774-4117/800-749-1687
Nera	800-774-4117/800-345-1612
Nice Systems	800-774-4117/800-345-1612
Nippon Telegraph	800-774-4117/800-749-1687
Norsk Hydro	800-774-4117/800-749-1687
Novo Nordisk	800-774-4117/800-749-1687
OzEMail	800-774-4117/800-345-1612
Pacific Dunlop	800-774-4117/800-749-1687
Petroleum Securities Australia	800-774-4117/800-345-1612
Rank Group	800-774-4117/800-749-1687
Repsol	800-774-4117/800-345-1612
Reuters Holdings	800-774-4117/800-749-1687
Ricoh Company	800-774-4117/800-345-1612
Royal Dutch Petroleum	800-774-4117/800-749-1687
Santos	800-774-4117/800-749-1687
Senetek	800-774-4117/800-345-1612
Sony Corp.	800-774-4117/800-749-1687
STET-Societa Finan. Telefonica	800-774-4117/800-749-1687
TAG Heuer International	800-774-4117/800-749-1687
TDK Corp.	800-774-4117/800-749-1687
Telecom Argentina STET-France Telecom	800-774-4117/800-749-1687
Telefonica del Peru	800-774-4117/800-749-1687
Telefonos de Mexico Series L	800-774-4117/800-749-1687
Thorn	800-774-4117/800-749-1687
Tubos de Acero de Mexico	800-774-4117/800-749-1687
Unilever NV	800-774-4117/800-749-1687
Unilever Plc	800-774-4117/800-749-1687
Unionamerica Holdings	800-774-4117/800-749-1687
Waterford Wedgwood	800-774-4117/800-749-1687
Westpac Banking	800-774-4117/800-749-1687
Xenova Group	800-774-4117/800-345-1612
Zeneca Group	800-774-4117/800-749-1687

Source: DRIP Investor.

ask for the names of financial planners in your area. You can also make your request through the home pages offered by ICFP (http://www.icfp.org) and NAPFA (http://www.feeonly.org). Favor advisers who seem to be both experienced and qualified, especially those holding the Certified Financial Planner (CFP) designation. Explain to the broker or planner that you are not going to buy any investments and that you are not looking for a full-blown financial plan, which can be horribly expensive. All you want to do is buy a few hours of his or her time, so that he or she can check that you have adequate insurance, a well-diversified portfolio, the right estate-planning documents and so on.

Brokers and financial planners are entrepreneurial types, so you probably won't have too much trouble finding someone to help. Draw up a detailed list of your portfolio holdings, insurance policies, debts outstanding, sources of income, annual amount saved and company benefits, so that the broker or planner doesn't waste hours figuring out what you have and instead spends the time analyzing your finances. Make sure the hourly fee—and the number of hours the broker or financial planner will take—is established ahead of time. These hours may prove expensive. But it will still be a lot cheaper than making year-round use of an investment adviser.

KEEP SIX MONTHS
OF EMERGENCY MONEY

Everybody should have some emergency money. This much I concede. But what about the received wisdom, which says you should have six months of living expenses sitting in a savings account or a certificate of deposit? I think it's utter bunk.

Sure, bad things happen. People get sick. Cars get totaled. Houses burn down. Folks lose their jobs. But do you realize how much money you need to cover six months of living expenses? If your household income is $60,000 a year, you might spend $3,000 a month on rent, food, clothes and other items. That's $18,000 for half a year.

Even if you are a committed saver, who socks away 10 percent of your pretax salary every month, it's going to take you three years to amass that money. Most folks, of course, don't save anything like 10 percent of their pretax salary. So if you hit that 10 percent target, you will probably do so only by sacrificing other goals, such as saving for a house down payment, or your kid's college, or your own retirement.

But finally, after three years of diligent savings, after night after night of leftovers and tuna fish sandwiches, you have your precious $18,000. At which point, according to the conventional wisdom, you should leave this princely sum sitting in a savings account or a money-market fund, where for the rest of your life the money will be ravaged by inflation and taxes. Absolutely absurd? Totally irrational? Completely inexplicable? Maybe we should just settle for "all of the above."

Where We Go Wrong

You won't achieve your financial goals—particularly retirement—if you don't behave like a long-term investor. Traditional company pensions are gone. Social Security will be cut back. Your lifestyle in retirement hinges on the size of your investment accounts. To make these accounts grow, you have to save regularly and invest aggressively, by putting money into stocks.

You also can't have it all. You cannot save for your own retirement, put your kids through expensive colleges, have a huge emergency reserve, help your parents financially, buy a house and own the full panoply of insurance. Some things have to give.

Which brings us back to the emergency-money rule of thumb, which states that you should keep six months of living expenses in conservative investments. If you are constantly in danger of getting laid off, maybe this rule really does make sense. But for the rest of us, I think it's ludicrous. You are committing a huge hunk of money to conservative investments to prepare for events that probably won't occur. After all, emergencies are, by definition, not something we expect to happen.

What's the alternative? Here's the less controversial solution. You could keep a smaller emergency reserve, maybe equal to only three months of living expenses. This sum is probably more than ample, especially when you consider the ease with which money can be borrowed to cover any shortfall. If you opt for the smaller emergency reserve, put a third of the money in a money-market fund and the other two-thirds in a short-term bond fund. These investments will give you more flexibility than a certificate of deposit, with which there are penalties for early withdrawals, and a higher yield than a savings account.

If an emergency strikes, tap your money-market fund first, because you can cash out shares without triggering a capital gain or loss. By contrast, you will have a capital gain or loss if you sell your short-term bond fund, and this transaction will then have to be reported on your next tax return. But as a reward for these tax hassles, the short-term bond fund should give you a higher return than a money-market fund.

Two caveats. First, make sure you keep all of your emergency money in a taxable account, not your retirement account. If you put emergency money in a retirement account and then have to tap the account, you will likely face income taxes on the amount withdrawn and probably a 10 percent tax penalty as well. Second, many mutual-fund companies will allow you to write checks against your short-term bond fund. But every time you write a check, you realize a capital gain or loss. If you write a dozen checks, that's a dozen taxable events, all of which then have to be reported on Schedule D of Internal Revenue Service Form 1040. Your accountant will adore you.

The New Rules

I think that putting three months of living expenses in conservative investments isn't a bad strategy for your emergency reserve. But it's not what I am doing. Instead, I have a small amount of my emergency money in cash investments—and the rest in stocks.

In June 1995, I described this strategy in my regular weekly column for *The Wall Street Journal*. The response was entirely gratifying. Abuse was heaped on me by some of Wall Street's self-appointed gurus. My old employer, *Forbes,* chose to criticize me in the magazine's pages not just once, but twice. "When mass circulation newspapers give their readers advice like that, a (market) top can't be far way," opined *Forbes* in its September 11, 1995, issue. The Standard & Poor's 500-stock index went on to gain almost 19 percent in the next 12 months. But even before the folks at *Forbes* started venting their spleens, a bunch of regular investors wrote and called, telling me that for years they had been following strategies similar to mine and that it was good to see somebody finally writing about it.

How does my strategy work? I keep some cash to cover small-scale disasters, like the pair of root canals that require urgent attention or the leak in the roof that's wrecking the bedroom ceiling. Smaller emergencies such as these shouldn't cost more than a few thousand dollars, so I keep at least that much in cash. After all, I don't want to be selling long-term investments every time the dishwasher dies.

Meanwhile, the rest of my emergency money is in a single well-diversified stock-mutual fund. Heresy? I don't think so. By putting my emergency money in stocks, I am not just preparing for the worst. I am also preparing for my retirement. Thanks to the superior returns earned by stocks, my emergency reserve should grow to far more than six months' living expenses and the money will eventually help to make my retirement even more comfortable. Who knows, maybe I will even be able to retire early. By contrast, if I left my emergency money in cash investments, it probably wouldn't grow at all, after inflation and taxes are figured in, and it certainly wouldn't make a meaningful contribution to my standard of living in retirement.

But what about the risks, you cry? My strategy is undoubtedly risky. If I get hit with a small-scale disaster, I can pay for it with my small pool of cash. But if I lose my job or get hit with a major medical bill, I could have to sell my stocks. That's fine if stocks are riding high. But my need to sell could coincide with a brutal bear market and I might be forced to sell shares at fire-sale prices.

I reduce a small amount of this risk by keeping my emergency money in a well-diversified stock fund, which includes a smattering of large-company stocks, small-company shares and foreign companies. Many of the major fund companies now offer these broadly diversified funds, which are often called lifecycle funds. Alternatively, if you have a large amount of emergency money, consider putting together a global portfolio of index funds. Index funds make relatively small capital-gains distributions each year, so they tend to be fairly tax-efficient and thus can be a good choice for a taxable account. Moreover, by owning a collection of funds, rather than a single lifecycle fund, you have more control over what to sell if you get hit with an emergency. If U.S. stocks are riding high while foreign stocks are in the dumps, you could choose to sell your U.S. stock-index fund to pay for the emergency, while leaving your foreign stock-index fund to recover.

But diversification can only do so much. By owning a broadly diversified stock fund, I reduce the chance that my emergency reserve will get badly sunk by a single rotten stock or a single rotten part of the market. But if we get a really brutal bear market, it's likely to be a global phenomenon, and large-company stocks, small-company shares and foreign companies will probably put on an alarming display of synchronized sinking. Moreover, it could be a mighty long time before these shares bounce back. After all, if you bought stocks just ahead of the 1973–74 bear market, the worst market drop since the Great Depression, it would have taken 3½ years to get back to even, as measured by the total return of the Standard & Poor's 500-stock index. Most emergencies demand somewhat prompter attention.

A fatal flaw? Not at all. If stocks are in a bear market, I have no intention of selling my stock fund. So how will I pay for my emergency? If I put my mind to it, I figure I can get my hands on a fair amount of money fairly quickly by tapping credit cards, the equity in my home and the money in my company's retirement-savings plan. I will borrow money to pay for the emergency and then pay off the debt either out of my paycheck or by selling stocks after the market recovers. Borrowing money is clearly costly. But over the long haul, the superior returns from stocks should more than compensate for any short-term borrowing costs.

Sound too risky for you? Consider tailoring my plan to your tolerance for risk. Maybe you could put more of your emergency money in a money-market fund and a short-term bond fund and somewhat less in stocks. Maybe you could buy a lifecycle fund that's lighter on stocks and longer on bonds. But whatever you do, don't leave six months of living expenses languishing in cash investments. You work hard every day. Make sure your emergency money does the same.

DEBT IS DANGEROUS

Going into debt is awful. Not going into debt can be even worse.

Let's face it, as much as we decry our nation's proclivity to borrow, a lot of debt gets put to good use. It is, after all, how we bought our homes, put our kids through college and purchased our cars. It would be nice to have paid cold cash. But if we operated on that basis, many of us would drive clunkers and live in rental properties, and a lot of 42-year-olds would be sitting around, waiting to start their freshman year at college.

Moreover, debt is a key tool in solving one of the nagging problems of the 1990s. How do you behave like a long-term investor—so that you're able to retire in comfort and put your kids through college—while still making sure that you can get your hands on cash when you need it? Debt can help. By ensuring that you have quick and easy access to other people's money, you don't have to keep so much of your own money sitting in cash.

So is debt dangerous? It all depends on whom you ask.

Where We Go Wrong

Saver or spender? Most folks can be slotted fairly easily into one camp or the other. And the spenders, it seems, are in the majority. Unfortunately, when it comes to their finances, far too many Americans are hopelessly out of control. They run up huge credit-card bills and then wait for the next credit-card solicitation to arrive, so they can start another tab. Banks seem more than happy to feed this frenzy of indebtedness. Sure, some of the borrowers default. But enough people pay the steep interest charges to compensate for the deadbeats. For the financially ill-disciplined, easy credit is clearly a disaster. For these folks, debt is undoubtedly dangerous.

But for those who have their finances under control, borrowed money can be a godsend. If you need a lot of money in a hurry, cash is usually readily available, especially if you have a clean credit record. It's certainly comforting to have a pile of emergency money sitting in the bank. But in a pinch, a line of credit can be just as good.

Yet the financially prudent, who are most likely to use debt responsibly, are also those most reluctant to borrow. Some conservative investors steer clear of all debt. They don't even want to be tempted, so they avoid setting up a home-equity line of credit and they get irritated when the credit-card company raises their borrowing limit. Such sentiments are admirable, to be sure. But they could come back to haunt you.

I believe you should do everything possible to ensure easy access to money, just in case disaster strikes. No, you don't really want to borrow money. But suppose an emergency does arise. Maybe you don't have a lot of cash. Maybe your stocks and bonds, which you had planned on selling, are in the midst of a brutal bear market. You certainly don't want to offload these securities until prices have bounced back. So what do you do? Borrow.

Some sources of borrowing don't involve a lot of questions about employment, credit history and so on. But some do. Credit may be readily available in America. But often it's only available to folks who don't really need it. That's why you should arrange your credit lines now, before you lose your job and the bank decides you are a bad risk.

The New Rules

So what should you do if you get hit with an emergency and need some quick cash? If you can't tap your portfolio because stocks and bonds are in a swoon or you would simply prefer to borrow, here's where to turn.

Margin Accounts

Margin accounts, which allow you to borrow against the value of your investment portfolio, suggest images of devastated investors wiped out by collapsing markets. It doesn't have to be that way, however, if you use these accounts carefully.

If you want to borrow on margin, your investments have to be in a taxable account, not a retirement account. In addition, you have to hold your investments at a brokerage firm, rather than at a mutual-fund company. That's unfortunate, because mutual funds—including stock mutual funds—are ideal collateral for a margin account. Unlike individual stocks, which can fall precipitously, most stock funds move fairly sedately. What to do? If you are buying no-load mutual funds from a bunch of fund companies, consider investing through one of the mutual-fund supermarkets operated by discount brokers such as Fidelity Brokerage Services, Charles Schwab Corporation and Jack White & Co. Not only will you get the convenience of one-stop shopping, but you will also get to borrow on margin.

With a margin account, you can borrow up to half the value of most mutual funds at a low interest rate. But I think borrowing that much is far too risky. If you borrow half, you would get a margin call if your securities fell by 29 percent. While that's a huge drop, it's not unthinkable. When you receive a margin call, you have to pay back part of your margin loan or add more securities or cash to your account. If you don't, the brokerage firm will trim your margin debt by selling some of your securities, which has the effect of locking in the losses on those investments. That, of course, is when folks start jumping out of windows.

So how much should you borrow? Limit yourself to 20 percent of the account balance. If you borrowed 20 percent, your mutual funds and other investments would have to fall more than 70 percent before you got a margin call. I am not saying it couldn't happen. But if mutual funds are losing 70 percent of their value, something pretty dreadful has afflicted the world and the state of your investment account is probably the least of your worries.

Home-Equity Lines of Credit

Banks prefer to lend to folks who don't really need the money. So if you want to set up a home-equity line of credit, now is the time to do it, before disaster strikes. Once you have lost your job, the bank won't be nearly so accommodating. Moreover, setting up a home-equity line of credit is surprisingly involved. You need to fill out application forms, send the bank a slug of documents and get your house appraised. Once the credit line is approved, you usually have to meet at a lawyer's office to close on the line of credit, just as you did when you closed on your house.

But it can all be worth it, if you find yourself with an urgent need for money down the road. The interest rate on home-equity loans is low and the interest is usually tax-deductible. Often you don't have to pay anything to set up these credit lines—no appraisal fees, no application fees, no lawyers' fees. Some banks do stick customers with these costs, in return for which you usually pay a lower interest rate on any borrowing. But because your intention is never to use this credit line—you only want it for emergencies—I would go for the no-fee loan and take the risk of having to pay a slightly higher interest rate.

Your 401(k) or 403(b) Plan

Your biggest asset may well be the money sitting in your 401(k) or 403(b) retirement-savings plan. Ideally, you don't want to touch these accounts until you retire. But if you have to crack your retirement nest egg, your employer's plan can often provide you with quick cash. How do you tap these accounts? The trick is to avoid actually withdrawing money and instead to borrow.

In any case, Uncle Sam doesn't allow you to withdraw from a 401(k) or 403(b) plan, except under special circumstances. What qualifies? Among other things, you can make hardship withdrawals to buy a house, pay for college, cover medical costs or pay funeral expenses. The real hardship, however, is the cost involved. Even if you do qualify for a hardship withdrawal, you still have to pay income taxes on the amount involved and probably a 10 percent tax penalty as well. If you are in the 28 percent marginal tax bracket, that means losing 38 cents out of every dollar to the Internal Revenue Service.

You can't avoid the income taxes. Usually, you also can't avoid the 10 percent penalty, which gets slapped on almost any withdrawal from a retirement account before age 59½. It doesn't matter whether the money is coming out of a 401(k) plan, a 403(b) plan or an individual retirement account. But there are a few exceptions. For instance, you avoid the penalty if you become permanently disabled. You also sidestep the penalty if the money withdrawn is used to pay for that portion of your annual medical expenses that exceeds 7.5 percent of your adjusted gross income, as defined by the IRS. In addition, you can get money out of your employer's plan without paying a penalty if you leave your job and you are 55 or older. To avoid the penalty, you must take the money out of your employer's plan before you roll it over to an IRA. Once the money is in an IRA, you can't use this penalty-free withdrawal method.

Most of the time, however, withdrawing money from a 401(k) or 403(b) plan before age 59½ is a lousy idea, because of the taxes and penalties involved. End of story? Not at all. Forget about withdrawing money and consider taking out a loan instead.

By law, you can borrow half of your retirement-plan balance, up to $50,000. The loan has to be repaid within five years, unless the money is used to purchase a house, in which case there's no legal limit on the borrowing period. Sound like a good deal? Before you get too excited, check your employee handbook. Many employers impose stricter rules than those outlined in the law. For instance, your employer may not allow borrowing or may limit all loans to five years, including loans to home buyers.

In addition, your employer may insist that all loans be repaid if you leave the company. This provision—which many employers enforce—can wreak havoc. Indeed, you shouldn't take out a 401(k) loan if you think your job is in danger. If you get laid off and you can't immediately repay your loan, the borrowed money will be treated as a retirement-account distribution and will be subject to income taxes and maybe a 10 percent penalty. An un-

Saving for Retirement, Preparing for the Worst

Worried about losing your job? If your employer's retirement-savings plan allows it, consider making contributions that aren't tax-deductible, thereby building your own unemployment fund.

When you leave your employer, you may be able to leave these nondeductible contributions in your company's plan, if that's what you want. That way, your contributions will continue to grow tax-deferred, along with your other retirement savings. But if you need the money, just ask your employer to roll over your retirement-plan balance.

Arrange for all your tax-deductible contributions, all your employer's contributions and all of the account's investment gains to go directly to an individual retirement account or to your new employer's plan. What about your nondeductible contributions? Your employer will return those to you. You are then free to spend this money, without incurring income taxes or tax penalties. The money could come in handy, especially if it takes you a while to land a new job.

avoidable problem? If you are changing jobs, you may be able to roll over your retirement-account balance into your new employer's plan and then immediately borrow against it. In the intervening weeks, between the time you leave your old employer and the time you can start borrowing from your new plan, you will probably have to take out a temporary loan from the neighborhood bank. But if that allows you to skirt a huge tax bill, the borrowing cost involved would be well worth it.

Retirement-plan loans are great if you get hit with an emergency. But don't make them a habit. Many folks believe that borrowing from their employer's plan is a winning proposition, because the interest they pay on the loan goes into their account, so that they are effectively paying interest to themselves. But the fact is, when you take out a retirement-plan loan, you lose the investment earnings on the money borrowed. Indeed, the investment earnings forgone are the real borrowing cost. Missing out on investment gains may seem less painful than, say, paying interest to the bank. But the loss is just as real.

Individual Retirement Accounts

Unlike your home, your taxable investments and your employer's retirement-savings plan, an individual retirement account is not an asset you can borrow against. But if you get hit with an emergency, your IRA could still come in handy. In a pinch, it's possible to get money out of an individual retirement account before age 59½ without paying the 10 percent tax penalty.

You can pull money out of an IRA or out of an old employer's plan and avoid tax penalties, if you take the money out in "substantially equal periodic payments" over your life expectancy. Once you start, you have to keep pulling out money every year for five years or until you turn 59½, whichever is longer. Using this provision, you can tap your IRA at any age. But I wouldn't use this option unless you are at least age 50. Partly that's because you shouldn't be cracking open your retirement accounts any earlier than that. But also, the older you are, the shorter your life expectancy and hence the more money you can pull out each year

using substantially equal periodic payments. There are three different methods you can use to figure out how much to withdraw, and two of the methods can generate surprisingly large annual payouts. But the penalty for getting the calculation wrong is huge, so don't do this without consulting a good accountant or financial planner.

You can also make penalty-free withdrawals from an IRA to pay college expenses, buy your first home, pay huge medical bills or buy medical insurance if you become unemployed.

To make a penalty-free withdrawal to pay for medical expenses, you must be paying for costs that, during the course of the calendar year, exceed 7.5 percent of your adjusted gross income. If you pull the money out of a regular IRA, you will have to report the withdrawal as income on your tax return, though you should also be able to itemize your medical expenses and thus offset your IRA income with this tax deduction. You don't, however, have to take the itemized deduction in order to avoid the penalty.

Similarly, if you are unemployed, you may be able to make penalty-free IRA withdrawals to pay for medical insurance. To avoid the 10 percent tax penalty, you need to have collected unemployment compensation for at least 12 weeks either in the year of the withdrawal or in the year before the withdrawal.

Once every 12 months, you can also pull money out of your IRA temporarily. If you don't reinvest the money within 60 days, however, you get hit with taxes and penalties. Because of the quick repayment period, this doesn't seem like a great way to get emergency money. But hey, you never know. Maybe your IRA will provide the bridge loan that helps you buy a new house or survive a temporary cash crunch.

Cash-Value Life Insurance

I am not crazy about cash-value life insurance, which comes in three basic flavors, whole life, universal life and variable life. These policies, which provide a death benefit while also acting as an investment account, tend to be inordinately expensive. But if you have one of these policies and you have built up some cash

value, it can be a good source of money if you get hit with an emergency. You can borrow against the cash value and, in some cases, even withdraw your accumulated premiums tax-free.

Credit Cards

Margin accounts, home-equity loans, retirement accounts and life insurance all provide low-cost ways to borrow. Yet most folks steer clear of these options and instead plunk for credit-card debt, which often carries interest rates of 18 percent and above. What gives? Investors divide their money into different mental accounts. Because mutual funds, cash-value life insurance and houses are all seen as ways of accumulating wealth, folks don't like to borrow from them, so they reach for their credit cards instead.

Resist this impulse. If you have to borrow, look first to margin accounts, retirement accounts and other low-cost options. But if you have no other choice, credit cards will have to do. Consider getting a no-fee, low-interest card, such as those offered by AFBA Industrial Bank (800-776-2265) or USAA Federal Savings Bank (800-922-9092). If you are an Internet user and you want to find more low-cost cards, try Bank Rate Monitor (http://www.bank rate.com) or RAM Research (http://ramresearch.com). *The Wall Street Journal* also prints a list of low-cost credit cards once a month. Alternatively, go to the library and leaf through back issues of *Kiplinger's Personal Finance* or *Money* magazine. Both publications regularly publish information on low-cost credit cards.

Even with lower-cost cards, the interest charged can seem pretty steep. But if borrowing every so often against a credit card is the price you have to pay for holding less in cash and keeping the bulk of your emergency, retirement and college money in stocks, it's a price that is worth paying. The superior long-run returns you will get with stocks will easily justify the cost of carrying a balance on your credit cards every so often.

BUY THE BIGGEST HOUSE POSSIBLE

Combine brick, mortar and aluminum siding with lots of debt. Stir vigorously. Result? America's favorite investment.

Throughout this book, we've taken investments and investment strategies and tried to look at them rationally. So think long and hard. What do you really get when you buy a house? And why is this costly heap of headaches supposedly such a great investment?

Sure, a home does provide its owners with shelter and a pleasant sense of pride and security. But a house isn't a vibrant part of the economy. It doesn't grow. Unless you rent out a few rooms, your house doesn't provide goods or services that are sold to the wider community. Instead, it just sits there, eating up your home-improvement dollars and costing you real-estate taxes. How could something so prosaic make you wealthy? And yet, for an entire generation, the road to riches could be summed up in one simple dictum: Buy the biggest house possible.

It was certainly true for my parents. Lured by a lucrative job, my cash-strapped, thirtysomething father and twentysomething mother moved from London to Washington, D.C., in 1966. Once there, they cobbled together a $4,500 down payment so they could buy a $45,000 newly constructed, split-level house. Some 28 years later, in 1994, after my parents had divorced and the four kids had split, my father sold the house for $360,000.

Those were the good old days.

The lesson sure wasn't wasted on my generation. Scrape together a down payment, take out the largest mortgage possible and buy the biggest house you can. You will live rent-free and you will grow rich. You will feast on the mortgage-interest tax deduction. And if you don't really like the place, you can always trade up later.

So my friends rushed to buy real estate in the late 1980s, purchasing tiny New York apartments they could barely afford and rundown suburban homes that should have been called handyman specials, but weren't. And they lost their shirts. Some bailed out, losing their down payment and more. They quickly discovered that their losses had an added sting. Unlike failed stock and bond-market investments, real-estate losses aren't tax-deductible. Meanwhile, other friends are still toughing it out, desperate for more space and a better place, but too deeply in the hole to move.

Unlike our friends, my wife and I didn't lose our shirts. We weren't smarter or luckier than our friends, however. We were just more broke. We would have bought real estate too, but my wife was in graduate school, so we couldn't possibly afford a house. It was the smartest move we never made.

Where We Go Wrong

Why did my friends' homes turn into houses of horror? Real estate is usually a pretty good investment. But nowhere is it decreed that buying a huge house will make you rich. Indeed, what happened in the 1970s and early 1980s was something of an aberration. House prices enjoyed a huge spike, partly because of rising wages and surging demand as baby boomers entered the housing market. But inflation was the great elixir.

Through the 1970s and early 1980s, inflation was rampant, with consumer prices rising more than 10 percent in some years. As you might recall from earlier chapters, rapidly rising consumer prices are bad for financial assets like stocks and bonds. Indeed, both stocks and bonds were rotten investments throughout the 1970s.

But while inflation can be devastating for financial assets, it's great for so-called hard assets, like gold and collectibles and real estate. Over long periods, these hard assets may not make you much money, once inflation is figured in. But because hard assets are very good at holding their value relative to inflation, investors tend to flock to them at times of rapid consumer price increases.

So it was in the 1970s and early 1980s. As inflation drove up housing prices, homeowners enjoyed astonishing gains. Imagine you bought a $100,000 house with $20,000 down. Inflation then jumps 60 percent and your home's price follows suit, rising to $160,000. Result? Your home is worth no more in real, inflation-adjusted dollars. Only its nominal value has increased.

But if you bought the house with borrowed money, nominal increases are enough to make you rich. If inflation surges 60 percent and your home's nominal value posts a comparable gain, your wealth will balloon, because now you own a far bigger portion of the house. Instead of having $20,000 of equity in a $100,000 home, you have an $80,000 stake in a $160,000 house. Your equity share has gone from 20 percent to 50 percent.

The big loser, of course, is the bank that holds your mortgage. It lent you $80,000, which you are now repaying with dollars that, because of inflation, are worth a lot less than the dollars you originally borrowed. Indeed, in the 1970s and early 1980s, many homeowners effectively paid negative interest rates, because the rate charged on their mortgage was less than the inflation rate.

This mathematical magic enriched millions of Americans. The bigger your house and the more you had borrowed, the richer you got. But then, just as my friends were arriving at the party, something dreadful happened. Inflation disappeared, or almost.

The boom in real estate went bust, and my friends went bust, too. The math that worked so well for my parents' generation went into rapid reverse. That $20,000, which you put down on the $100,000 house, may have multiplied rapidly when house prices were going up. But when house prices fall, you stand to suffer the full loss. As your home's value slips to $90,000 and then $80,000, your $20,000 down payment is wiped out.

The New Rules

Because most of us borrow money to buy a house, we reap huge gains when the inflation rate and home prices rise and we suffer horribly when they fall. It's all a bit of a crapshoot. Maybe you will make out like a bandit, but maybe you won't.

This chance of huge gains, and risk of horrific losses, stems from the combustible mix of borrowed money and nominal gains or losses in a home's value. What happens if you strip away inflation from these nominal returns and just look at the real, inflation-adjusted gains? It turns out that houses are not a great source of appreciation. Over the long haul, your home's value will probably climb at about two percentage points a year more than inflation, so that if inflation checks in at 3 percent a year, your house might rise 5 percent or so.

That, in fact, is pretty much what happened with my parents' home. Sure, they put down $4,500 and eventually pocketed $360,000. But the $4,500 was the down payment on a $45,000 home; over the next three decades, they paid the rest of the house's purchase price—as well as considerable interest—through month after month of mortgage payments. The actual appreciation over the 28 years was from $45,000, the home's original price, to $360,000. That's equal to a 7.7 percent annualized rate of return. In the same period, inflation clocked in at 5.6 percent a year and stocks climbed 11 percent annually. The house, which had benefited from the booming Washington real-estate market and the nationwide surge in home prices through the 1970s and much of the 1980s, had gained barely two percentage points a year more than inflation. Indeed, the parental split-level couldn't even keep up with stocks.

Maybe you are starting to think that houses aren't that good an investment. Not true. If you are like many folks, your house will probably still turn out to be one of your better investments. But it's not because an inflationary wave is just around the corner. Rather, your home will turn out to be a wonderful investment because—regardless of what happens to inflation—owning a home forces you to save. Every month, with every mortgage check, you come to own a little bit more of your house. After 15, 20 or 30 years on the installment payment program, you will be the outright owner of a substantial asset.

Sound attractive? Consider the implications. If your goal is to build up a lot of home equity quickly, buying the biggest house possible may not be the best strategy. True, purchasing a bigger house forces you to make bigger monthly mortgage payments and, if inflation surges, you will do very nicely.

But without that surge of inflation, buying that big house isn't the quickest way to build home equity. After all, if you buy a big house, you will have to take out a big mortgage, with payments that stretch over 30 years. In the first 15 years of the mortgage, you hardly pay down any of the mortgage's principal balance. For instance, if you borrowed $300,000 using a 30-year fixed-rate mortgage with a 7 percent interest rate, you would have just $78,000 of the loan paid off after 15 years.

So what should you do if you want to accumulate home equity in a hurry? Richard T. Garrigan and Joseph L. Pagliari, Jr. ("Housing Appreciation, Income Taxes, and Mortgage Alternatives," *Real Estate Review,* Summer 1995), argue that you should buy a slightly smaller house and take out a 15-year mortgage, so that you own the house free and clear in 15 years. Alternatively, rather than using a 15-year loan to buy the slightly smaller home, you could take out a 30-year mortgage and then make extra-mortgage payments. The interest rate on a 30-year mortgage will be somewhat higher than that on a 15-year mortgage. But some home buyers, who can afford the larger payments demanded by a

15-year mortgage, plunk for the 30-year mortgage instead, so that they won't be locked into the larger payments. These folks often end up making larger payments anyway, so that they pay off their mortgage early.

Making extra-mortgage payments or taking out a 15-year mortgage are both surefire strategies for quickly accumulating lots of home equity. Intrigued? It's time for Myth No. 18.

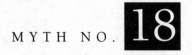

YOU CAN'T BEAT THE MORTGAGE TAX DEDUCTION

Americans hate to pay taxes, which is one of the reasons they love their homes. The mortgage-interest deduction is one of the last great tax breaks and many folks just can't get enough of it. Indeed, lots of people buy absurdly big houses so they can take out absurdly big mortgages and thus have absurd amounts of mortgage interest to deduct on their tax return.

This is absurd.

In Myth No. 17, I argued that buying the biggest house possible isn't always a great idea. The same holds true for taking out a big mortgage. You may have been told that a big mortgage is the road to riches. But the fact is, those interest payments are costing you a lot more than they are costing Uncle Sam.

Where We Go Wrong

Admittedly, deducting mortgage interest used to be a far more attractive proposition. Back in the late 1970s, when the highest-income earners got taxed at a marginal rate of over 50 percent, tax-deductible mortgage interest really was a great deal for those who pulled down big salaries. You might pay one dollar in interest, but that interest could be worth more than 50 cents in tax savings. After figuring in this tax savings, homeowners often found that their mortgage rate was substantially below the prevailing inflation rate. It was like stealing candy from a baby, but you were stealing from the bank, which made it even sweeter.

Today, however, the top tax rates aren't nearly so punishing. Most Americans, in any case, get taxed at marginal rates of 15 percent or 28 percent, which severely crimps the value of any tax deduction. If you send one dollar of mortgage interest to the bank, you will save 15 cents or 28 cents in taxes. The other 85 cents or 72 cents? Unfortunately, that comes out of your wallet. That's right, all that mortgage interest isn't saving you a whole lot in taxes, but it's costing you a small fortune.

What if your income is taxed at a marginal rate of more than 28 percent? If you earn a lot of money and you itemize your deductions when you file your tax return, you may have noticed that Schedule A isn't what it used to be. Schedule A is where you list all your itemized deductions, including medical expenses, state and local taxes, real-estate taxes, mortgage interest and charitable gifts. But if you earn a six-figure salary, the value of some of your itemized deductions—including the mortgage interest—can be severely curtailed.

The news gets worse. For all indebted homeowners, the biggest potential tax break from your mortgage comes in the early years, because that's when you pay the most interest. Every mortgage payment you send in gets split, so that some of the money goes toward interest payments and some pays off the loan's principal balance. In the early years of the mortgage, very little of your monthly payment goes toward principal and most of it goes toward interest. But as the years pass, the balance shifts, with more and more of each check going toward principal.

Why should you care about this? When you first buy a house and you have a lot of tax-deductible mortgage interest, you are probably early in your career, your salary is fairly low and you aren't in a particularly high tax bracket. All of which means the oodles of tax-deductible mortgage interest aren't saving you a whole lot in taxes.

A few years down the road, your salary will be higher and your tax bracket will be more impressive. But by then, even though you are making the same mortgage payment every month, more of it is going toward principal and less toward interest. Just when that tax-deductible mortgage interest might be really valuable, you are getting less of it.

Indeed, at some point, all that tax-deductible mortgage interest could be utterly useless. How so? As your annual mortgage interest shrinks, you may find that your total itemized deductions aren't that great and you are better off taking the standard deduction. For those filing in early 1998, for instance, the standard deduction is $6,900 for couples filing jointly and $4,150 for single individuals. Some 75 percent of tax filers take the standard deduction.

Contrary to what a lot of folks believe, you can't get rich taking tax deductions. This is true for deducting medical expenses, it's true for deducting state, local and real-estate taxes, it's true for mortgage interest and it's true for charitable gifts (not that I want to discourage charitable giving). Tax deductions don't save you money. They cost you money. You spend one dollar, but you might save just 15 or 28 cents in taxes. The only exception is tax-deductible retirement-account contributions. With these retirement-account contributions, you still get the tax savings, but instead of spending the money, you invest it. It's a win-win proposition. But with every other type of tax deduction, you lose more than you gain. You spend a slug of money, but you save only a sliver in taxes.

Tax-deductible mortgage interest? Who needs it?

The New Rules

After a while, you may get tired of the monthly payments, you realize that this whole mortgage business is a waste of money and you decide to pay off the damn thing. Indeed, every so often, when I feel brave, I write a column for *The Wall Street Journal* in which I suggest that readers make extra-mortgage payments, so that they pay off their mortgage more quickly. Then the phone rings and rings and the letters pour in and I realize how dumb it is to be brave. When it comes to mortgages, a lot of folks just can't think straight.

There are some perfectly sound arguments for not paying down your mortgage. But believe me, there are also some mighty dumb reasons why folks don't make extra-mortgage payments. Have you been told that you should never, ever, ever pay down your mortgage? It's time somebody put you right.

Here's how to decide whether to make extra-mortgage payments. First, find out what the interest rate is on your mortgage. Let's say it's 7.5 percent. That's how much you effectively earn by making extra-mortgage payments, because that's the interest expense you avoid.

Now ask yourself, "What would I do with the money, if I didn't make extra-mortgage payments?" Lots of things will earn you a higher return than that 7.5 percent. For instance, you could get a better return by paying off your credit cards, which might be charging you 18 percent. Over the long haul, you should also earn more than 7.5 percent by buying stocks.

What if your taste runs to bonds, money-market funds and certificates of deposit? Now it gets trickier. In all likelihood, the interest rate on your mortgage is higher than the yield on these investments, which suggests that you should pay down your mortgage. On the other hand, your mortgage interest is tax-deductible. For instance, if you are in the 15 percent bracket, your 7.5 percent mortgage is really costing you 6.38 percent. For those in the 28 percent bracket, the real cost is even lower, just 5.4 percent.

The fact that your mortgage interest is tax-deductible doesn't matter, however, if the alternative is to invest through a taxable account. After all, if you are in the 28 percent bracket, the real cost of your 7.5 percent mortgage may be only 5.4 percent. But if instead of paying down your mortgage, you buy a 7 percent bond in your taxable account, you will be worse off. After you pay the

Myth Busting in Mortgage Land

Many folks adamantly refuse to pay down their mortgage, even though it would be the best use of their money. They regularly shovel cash into savings accounts that pay 2 percent, believing it's a better investment than paying off their 7.5 percent mortgage. These are the victims of the mortgage myths. They believe that they don't save any interest when they make extra-mortgage payments or, if they do save money, it's only a very small amount.

These befuddled homeowners typically have fixed-rate mortgages. With an adjustable-rate mortgage, in which the interest rate charged fluctuates every year, you see the benefits of making extra-mortgage payments very quickly. If you make extra payments, the bank figures this into its annual recalculation, so that the extra-mortgage payments work to reduce your required monthly payment. But be warned: When the bank next recalculates your mortgage, the annual payment won't always go down, even if you have made extra payments. If interest rates have gone up, the bank will increase the interest charged on your mortgage and this could swamp the impact of your extra payments.

But barring sharp interest-rate increases, with an adjustable-rate mortgage you should see the benefit of your extra-mortgage payments fairly quickly. Not so with a fixed-rate mortgage. With a fixed-rate mortgage, nothing seems to come of your extra payments, because these extra payments don't reduce your required monthly payment. Instead, when you make extra payments on a fixed-rate mortgage, you shorten the length of the mortgage. And therein lies a whole heap of confusion.

The most befuddled homeowners think they don't save any interest when they make extra-mortgage payments and that the money simply reduces the amount of principal that's owed to the bank. But more commonly, folks think they are saving some interest, but not very much. How come? As you pay down your mortgage, the balance between interest and principal shifts, so that an increasing amount goes toward principal each month and less goes toward interest. The result is that, in the later years of the mortgage, very little interest is charged and most of your monthly payment goes toward principal.

Some homeowners look at that and figure there's no point in making extra-mortgage payments, because all you do is avoid payments in the later years of your mortgage, when you don't get charged much interest anyway. That, however, is not the way it works. In effect, when you make extra-mortgage payments, it's not the later years of the mortgage you avoid, but the early years, when a lot of interest is charged.

Maybe an example will help. Suppose you have just taken out a $200,000, 30-year mortgage that carries an 8 percent interest rate. The monthly payment is $1,467.53. How much would you have to add to your first mortgage payment to avoid the last one? Just $135. That's right, to avoid paying $1,467.53 in 30 years, all you have to do is pay $135 today. What explains the difference between $135 and $1,467.53? That's the interest you save.

If you want to try this sort of calculation yourself, get hold of one of the personal-finance software programs. Alternatively, play with the mortgage calculator offered on the Internet by financial publisher HSH Associates (http://www.hsh.com). HSH, as well as Bank Rate Monitor (http://www.bankrate.com), can also help in identifying low-rate mortgages.

tax on your bond's 7 percent yield, you will be left with just over 5 percent, which is less than the 5.4 percent you could earn by paying down your mortgage.

But what if, instead of purchasing that 7 percent bond in your taxable account, you buy it in a tax-deferred account, like a 401(k) plan, a Keogh or an individual retirement account? In that case, you are better off buying the 7 percent bond, because you don't pay tax on the interest each year, though you will have to pay income tax when the money is eventually withdrawn from the account (unless the money is coming out of one of the new Roth IRAs). Investing through the tax-deferred account is an especially good choice if your contributions are tax-deductible or if you are funding a Roth IRA. In addition, if you are investing through a 401(k) or similar employer-sponsored plan, you may get some sort of matching contribution from your employer.

My advice: Don't make extra-mortgage payments if instead you will pay off higher-interest debt, buy stocks or invest through a retirement account. But if the alternative is to buy conservative investments in a taxable account, you are probably better off making extra-mortgage payments.

Home Free

If you do decide to pay down your mortgage, you will find there are some great benefits:

■ You know exactly how much you will earn. If you have a 7.5 percent mortgage, that 7.5 percent is what you save by making extra-mortgage payments. By contrast, if you bought, say, a bond with a 7.5 percent yield, you can't be nearly so sure of earning 7.5 percent. The bond's issuer could default on its interest payments or interest rates could rise, driving down your bond's price. Moreover, paying down your mortgage doesn't involve the need for any investment research. Meanwhile, researching the bonds—or any other investment, for that matter—could involve untold hours at the library or talking to a broker or financial planner.

■ Paying down your mortgage is easy. All you have to do is throw in a few extra dollars when you write your monthly mortgage check. Many folks simply round up the dollar amount, so that the $1,467.53 mortgage payment becomes $1,500.

Some banks offer so-called biweekly mortgages with which, instead of paying once a month, you pay half that amount every two weeks. The net result is that you make 26 biweekly payments each year, rather than 12 monthly payments, so you effectively end up making an extra monthly payment during the year. Biweekly plans are okay, providing you don't have to pay the bank anything to set them up and providing you can get out of the plans at short notice. But if your bank charges for setting up the service—my mortgage provider wanted some $300—skip it and stick to adding money to your regular monthly payment.

■ You buy yourself some substantial financial freedom.

Once your mortgage is paid off, you will still have to pay your real-estate taxes and buy home insurance. But the big monthly payment will be gone, freeing up money each month that you could put toward your kid's college tuition or that may allow you to work part-time or not at all. With your mortgage out of the way, you also won't have to hold nearly so much emergency money.

Even before you have paid off your mortgage completely, you will have built up substantial home equity, which you can then borrow against to pay college-tuition bills or tide you over while you find another job. As soon as you have a fair amount of home equity built up, consider setting up a home-equity line of credit. Many folks don't like to pay down their mortgage, because they feel they won't have ready access to the money if they get hit with a financial emergency. Clearly, if you have a sudden need for cash, you can't sell your house, as you could your investments. But if you have a home-equity line of credit, your money will be as readily available as if it were sitting in a bank account or a mutual fund.

INVEST IN YOUR HOUSE

Owning your own home is the American dream. Or at least that's what the real-estate broker told us when my wife and I finally got around to buying a house. But it sure didn't seem that way when, a few days after we closed, we discovered sewage spewing into the basement. We were eventually able to flush the toilet with impunity, but only after the plumber had ripped up the front lawn, replaced the root-infested sewer pipe and relieved us of $1,200.

Houses aren't a dream. They're a nightmare. Every home-owner knows that houses swallow money, great quantities of dollars that fly from your checkbook whenever the plumbing springs a leak or the boiler needs replacing. Yet homeowners persist in believing that, when they have their house painted every decade or the roof replaced every 25 years or a new kitchen put in, they are investing in their home.

Of course, if you didn't paint your house or fix the roof or upgrade the kitchen, your house would start to look like a dump and life would become increasingly uncomfortable. But are these

improvements and repairs really an investment? The whole notion is laughable.

Where We Go Wrong

Homes are peculiar, because they straddle the worlds of investment and consumption. Indeed, I think a lot of the odd thinking about real estate occurs for this very reason. It's tough to love
a mutual fund, but it's easy to love your house. We like the idea of
buying homes, fixing them up and trading up to bigger places. We
want to believe that we are doing all this because real estate is a
great investment. But we are really doing it because we like it.

Nowhere is this clearer than with major home improvements. We enjoy putting in the new kitchen or adding on a garage
or enclosing the sun room and turning it into a playroom for the
kids. We justify spending the money by saying it's an investment.
But is it?

Of course not. The idea that home improvements and repairs are an investment is part wishful thinking, part financial il-
lusion. We really want the new kitchen, so we go looking for the
justification. And the justification seems to be there. You buy a
house for $150,000 and later sell it for $220,000. Why did the
house appreciate? It must have been your tasteful home improvements, right? Wrong.

Over the long haul, your home's value might climb at two
percentage points a year more than inflation, so that if inflation
runs at 3 percent a year over the next decade, you could reason-
ably expect to earn 5 percent. But the reason your home's value
climbs faster than inflation isn't that everybody just loves your
decorating touch, it's that the land underneath your home is so
valuable. We have a limited amount of land, a growing population
and, as we grow richer as a nation, a thirst for grander homes. All
of which means land values don't merely keep up with inflation,
but tend to rise a little faster.

But what about the building itself, on which you lavish your love and your dollars? The bitter truth is, it's a depreciating asset, which needs lots of tender love and affection and money just to maintain its value. If you didn't sink at least some dollars into maintaining your house, your property might not increase at two percentage points a year more than inflation. Sure, the land would keep gaining. But without a lot of expensive attention, the dwelling wouldn't hold its own relative to inflation, and your property's overall value would suffer.

The New Rules

Every year, you can expect maintenance expenditures equal to between 1 percent and 1.5 percent of your home's value. Included in this number is the sort of stuff you need to do just to ensure that your home keeps up with the general pace of increase in housing prices. If you have a $200,000 house, you are looking at an annual outlay of between $2,000 and $3,000. If your home is fairly new, the tab should be somewhat lower. But as your house ages, the annual hit tends to rise.

So does all this maintenance expenditure really count as an investment? On the one hand, you need to spend these dollars so that your home keeps appreciating along with other properties in the neighborhood. On the other hand, a lot of these expenditures arise because you don't simply invest in a house, as you do in a stock or a bond or a mutual fund. You also live in the place. You consume real estate. You wear out the property. And after the stuff gets worn out, you have to repair or replace it. Repairs are the price you pay for consuming real estate. As such, the costs involved are pretty much unavoidable.

That sure isn't true for home improvements, which eat up the really big bucks. So do these count as an investment? If you have any lingering doubts on that question, consider the widely cited annual survey put together by *Remodeling,* a monthly magazine based in Washington, D.C. The 1996 survey showed, among other things, that you might recoup 95 percent of the cost of a minor kitchen remodeling, 91 percent of a bathroom addition, 83 percent of a family-room addition, 77 percent of a bathroom re-modeling and 72 percent from adding on a deck.

Homeowners look at these statistics and they think the numbers justify all those expensive home improvements. But that's not what the numbers are saying at all. If you add a family room and you manage to recoup 83 percent of your money, that means you've lost 17 percent—which, in my humble opinion, makes it a lousy investment. Moreover, *Remodeling* magazine's estimates are based on selling your home within a year of making the improvement. The longer you wait to sell your house, the shabbier your improvements will look and the less you will recoup.

The reality is, when you undertake a major home improvement, you are not investing money, you are spending it. That's a perfectly reasonable thing to do, if the pleasure you get from the improvements matches the dollars you spend. But don't spend money on home improvements out of some deluded notion that they will turn out to be a good investment. It just isn't so.

The bottom line? Home improvements and repairs are a money loser. But that doesn't mean you shouldn't undertake them. You may never recoup the cost of fixing the kitchen faucet. But your home's resale value will suffer if you don't keep your house in good repair. You may never recoup the cost of remodeling the kitchen. But if you will thoroughly enjoy your new kitchen, it is money well spent.

Moreover, making major home improvements is sometimes the financially prudent thing to do. Why? By expanding and improving your home, you may be able to avoid trading up. Home improvements are typically a rotten investment. But trading up is often worse.

TRADE UP AS SOON AS YOU CAN

The conventional wisdom states that you should buy the biggest house you can and take out the largest mortgage possible. So you dig deep and stretch to buy that starter home. But after five or six years, if home prices have cooperated and your employer has been kind, you may find that you have a decent amount of home equity and a higher salary. The mortgage has become all too manageable. And you can't forget the golden rule of real estate, which maintains that bigger is always better. So why not boost your investment and trade up to an even larger place?

This reasoning is so flawed it's pitiful.

In our myth-busting, we have already seen that buying a big house and taking out a huge mortgage are not necessarily the road to riches. And clearly both those myths are used to justify trading up. But there are two other reasons why you should think long and hard before you buy a bigger home. First, it is obscenely expensive. Second, it's ridiculous to own a house that's far bigger than you really want or need. Let's take a look at both points.

Where We Go Wrong

If you sell a no-load mutual fund and buy another one, it costs you nothing. If you ask a discount broker to sell 100 shares of one large company and then purchase 100 shares of another blue-chip stock, you might lose something less than 2 percent of your money to commissions and trading spreads. But if you sell one house and then purchase a new one, you could end up saying good-bye to an amount equal to 10 percent of the first home's value.

Trading up is so expensive it's criminal. First, you have to sell your existing place, which means paying a real-estate broker's commission equal to 5 percent or 6 percent of your home's value. How did commissions ever come to be that high, and what keeps them at such exorbitant levels? That alone is worthy of a government investigation. Then there's the cost of buying the new place. You have to use a lawyer, take out title insurance, get the place appraised, surveyed and inspected and pay the mortgage-application fee. There are also a bunch of other irritating costs, including notary, recording and credit-report fees.

But when buying, your biggest single expense will probably be the up-front interest costs known as points, which might amount to 2 percent or 2.5 percent of the size of the mortgage on your new place. Put it all together and buying the new place could easily cost you an amount equal to between 3 percent and 5 percent of your old home's value. Add that to the 5 percent or 6 percent that you paid to the real-estate broker who sold your old house and you could be out 10 percent.

The expenses don't stop there. You haven't even paid the moving expenses or the redecorating costs that inevitably come with a new place. And then there are the bigger monthly mortgage payments and the higher maintenance costs and the heftier real-estate taxes and the bigger home-insurance bills.

It makes me sick just thinking about it.

The problem is, the real-estate market is horribly inefficient. If you sell 100 shares of IBM, the buyer knows exactly what he's getting. There's no need to look over the shares or have them inspected. Your round lot (as 100 shares are known) of IBM is just like anybody else's round lot. Not surprisingly, there aren't a lot of costs or hassles involved in selling IBM.

Meanwhile, however, every house is different. Even if you buy a split-level house in a planned community of split-level homes, there will still be variations among the houses. They will be on different plots of land with different views. The interiors will vary. Some of the houses will have been upgraded. Others will have been allowed to deteriorate. Because every house is different, buying and selling can never be terribly efficient, so it will almost always be terribly expensive.

Doing It All for Love

But just as home improvements are worth undertaking if you will really get a lot of pleasure from that new kitchen or that new deck, so it's worth trading up if you really want to live in a bigger house or a better neighborhood or a better school district. Unfortunately, however, lots of folks don't trade up because they want or need a bigger and better place. They trade up because they think they will make money.

Think of your house the way you would think of a stock. Your gain comes in two parts, the dividend and the capital appreciation. With a stock, the capital appreciation is the biggest component of your total return, while the dividend is less important. But with a house, just the opposite is true. Most of your gain comes in the form of a dividend.

This dividend is your so-called imputed rent, the fact that as a homeowner you get to live in a nice place without paying rent. Don't the mortgage payments count as rent payments, you ask? Not really. Mortgage payments are the cost you pay to buy a house, not to rent it. To be sure, one of the perks of buying a house is that you get to live in it. But you also benefit from any home-price appreciation and you gradually come to own the entire house free and clear. Indeed, once you have paid off the mortgage, you will still enjoy your home's imputed rent without paying anything every month. By contrast, when renters send in their monthly rent checks, they get the right to live in a house for one month and that's it.

The imputed rent you receive each year is probably equal to between 7 percent and 8 percent of your home's value. To get a handle on your home's dividend, think about how much you would get each year if you rented out your house. Living in the house yourself, however, usually makes much more economic sense. When you "rent to yourself," you don't have to pay income tax on the rent you effectively receive.

Typically, a home's capital appreciation isn't nearly as important as this dividend. As I have mentioned before, over the long haul, your home's value might climb at two percentage points a year more than inflation, so that if the long-run annual inflation rate turns out to be 3 percent, your house might rise 5 percent a year.

Put it all together and houses look pretty attractive, with maybe an 8 percent dividend and 5 percent capital appreciation, for a total return of 13 percent. That's more than investors have earned from stocks historically. But remember, there are a lot of expenses involved in home ownership, including maintenance costs, real-estate taxes and home insurance, not to mention the hefty costs of buying and selling. The larger your house and the more often you trade up, the bigger these costs will be.

Which brings us back to the notion that, if you are going to trade up, you should do it because you really want that bigger house and not because you think it's going to be a good investment. Think about the numbers again. The dividend is worth maybe 8 percent a year. The capital appreciation might add another 5 percent. So let's say you trade up because you think it's a good investment and you end up owning a huge house that you don't really appreciate. Your dividend is worth 8 percent a year to somebody. But it's clearly not worth 8 percent to you. In other words, it's as though you pay a lot in rent, but you only use half the house.

What about capital appreciation? If you own a $300,000 home and all house prices climb 5 percent, it's true you will make twice as much in dollar terms as somebody who owns a $150,000 home. But if you would be just as happy in a smaller house, you could take the money that you would otherwise put into real estate and put it into a short-term bond fund and make 5 percent a year with far less risk—and without all the maintenance, real-estate tax and home-insurance costs. And if you earned more than 5 percent, by buying stocks or longer-term bonds, you would be far better off. Your investment account's value would rise faster than real-estate prices and you wouldn't be wasting imputed rent.

The New Rules

When the boiler isn't broken and the roof isn't leaking, owning your own home can seem quite wonderful. It's a great pleasure to have your own place, decorate it, fix it up, share it with friends and family. But this has nothing to do with making money. Sure, it's nice if your house turns out to be a good investment. But that's not the reason you buy a house. Houses are more about consumption than investment. You should keep this in mind in all your real-estate dealings and all your home-improvement decisions.

So what sort of house should you buy? The answer is, you should buy a house that you really like and that you can see living in for the rest of your days. In an ideal world, you would purchase only one house in your life, so that you avoid the costly process of repeatedly buying and selling.

When you first buy, if you figure your income will rise and you want more house than you can really afford right now, consider stretching a little to buy the sort of house you really want. That way, you will avoid becoming quickly dissatisfied. On the other hand, don't stretch to buy a house if you are not confident that your job is safe and you are not sure that your income will grow. Your massive mansion, with mortgage payments to match, could become a millstone if you are laid off.

If you can't afford the house you really want, think about putting your plans on hold, while you save more and your salary rises. Alternatively, if you are determined to buy, consider purchasing a place that you can improve or add on to. Home improvements aren't a good investment. But adding on is often a lot cheaper than moving on. If you are going to follow the fix-up strategy, make sure you are fixing up a house that deserves all the attention. What you want is a house that is currently the eyesore of the neighborhood, but could be made to look just as good as its neighbors. Real-estate experts often warn against buying the best house on the block. By the same token, you also don't want to end up with the best house in the neighborhood because of elaborate home improvements.

If you do decide to trade up, don't automatically opt for another 30-year mortgage. If you had already paid off 10 years of your earlier 30-year mortgage, consider taking out a 20-year or even a 15-year mortgage when buying the new house. That way, the price of a bigger house won't turn out to be three decades of indentured servitude to your least favorite mortgage company.

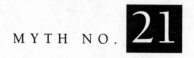

PROTECT AGAINST EVERY DISASTER

Insurance is a great idea. Except when it's not.

When you buy the right sort of insurance, it's one of the smartest moves you will ever make, because you will have protected yourself and your family against potentially devastating events. But when you buy the wrong type of insurance, it's like throwing your money away.

Distinguishing between the two is critical. I have said it before in this book and I will repeat it here: You have a limited amount of money to save and spend, and with that money you must meet some exceedingly costly financial goals, including buying a house, putting your kids through college and saving for your own retirement.

You may have been brought up to believe that you should buy insurance to protect against every eventuality. But the fact is, you can't afford to. You may be in the habit of buying insurance indiscriminately, never distinguishing between what's really necessary and what's not. But if you do that, you run the risk of ending up with inadequate coverage in critical areas. The consequences could be devastating.

Life Insurance

Extended warranties are the junkiest type of insurance. But fortunately, you don't need these policies. By contrast, you probably do need life insurance. Who doesn't? Life insurance shouldn't be bought by anybody who doesn't have true dependents. That means you don't need life insurance on your three-year-old daughter's life. I know the policies are cheap. Yes, you would suffer emotionally if she died. But insurance policies don't fix broken hearts. They fix broken bank balances. Nobody is financially dependent on your three-year-old daughter, so there's no reason to buy insurance on her life.

The same holds true if you are single with no dependents. Who is going to suffer financially if you die? Nobody, so you don't need life insurance. What if you are married? If you don't have kids and you both work, neither of you may need life insurance. A lot depends on whether you really rely on each other's income. Suppose you have a large monthly mortgage payment that neither you nor your spouse could afford if you were on your own. If that's the case, you probably need some life insurance.

Once kids arrive, everything changes and it's time to get heaps of life insurance. Your best bet is some cheap term insurance, which provides a death benefit and nothing more. What about cash-value life insurance, which is a lot more expensive, because it combines an investment account with a death benefit? We will get to the debate over cash-value life insurance later.

But the world of life insurance doesn't stop with term and cash-value life insurance. If you have ever taken out a loan, you may have been offered credit-life insurance, which would pay off the loan if you died. These policies, which sometimes don't involve a health examination, tend to attract folks who can't qualify for regular term or cash-value life insurance. As a result, the premiums are high and the policies aren't worth buying—unless, of course, you are one of those who can't qualify for regular life insurance.

I would also steer clear of so-called double-indemnity and triple-indemnity policy riders. These riders, which you usually pay extra for, will double or even triple your life insurance policy's death benefit if you are killed in an accident. I have never understood the point of double and triple indemnity. With insurance coverage, why does it matter whether you die in a car crash or you die in your sleep? One may be more gruesome than the other. But that sure doesn't change the financial needs of your family.

Similar reasoning applies with flight insurance. If you get to the airport and you are worried about what would happen to your beloved spouse and your lovely children should the plane go down in flames, it doesn't mean you need flight insurance. It means you should take the time to figure out whether you have enough regular life insurance.

Eventually, your kids will leave home and once again it will be just you and your spouse. By this point, you probably have a fair amount of assets. Would your spouse suffer financially if you died? If the answer is no, you don't need life insurance, unless you are using it for estate-planning purposes. More on that later.

Health Insurance

If you are abundantly rich and medical bills can be paid out of pocket change, don't worry about health insurance. You can "self-insure," which means you assume the risks associated with your own potential ill-health.

Most of us can't afford that risk, so, if we don't have health insurance through our employer, we buy private health insurance. If you can't afford a comprehensive health-care policy, which covers most medical and hospital bills, make sure you have basic health-care insurance that covers hospitalization. When you buy health insurance, you want coverage that, at a minimum, picks up that tab if you get hit with major medical expenses. What you don't want are policies that provide only partial benefits or only pay off in particular scenarios. For instance, many folks are drawn to dread-disease policies, which help with medical costs if you get a particular disease, usually cancer. But what if you have a heart attack? You are out of luck. Instead of buying dread-disease policies, put those dollars toward improving your basic health-care coverage.

Equally inadequate is hospital-indemnity insurance, which pays a fixed amount for every day you are in hospital. The policy might pay $100 a day, which isn't a lot of help when 24 hours in a hospital could easily run into thousands of dollars. Much hospital-indemnity insurance is sold to seniors, who would be much better off buying a decent Medigap policy. Medigap policies are specially designed to pick up the costs not covered by Medicare, the health program for those 65 and up.

Disability Insurance

Social Security will provide benefits if you are totally disabled. But it's tough to qualify for these disability benefits and, in any case, the Social Security payments probably won't come close to replicating your current salary. As a result, most folks need disability insurance. You may have coverage through your employer, so you don't even think about it. It's worth checking, however, that this coverage is adequate. Ideally, you want coverage that will replace your entire after-tax income. But typically, even the best coverage will replicate only 60 percent or 70 percent of your income. If these benefits come from an employer, they are less valuable. How so? Benefits from employer-purchased disability policies are taxable, while the benefits received from policies you buy yourself are tax-free.

If your employer's coverage is inadequate, or if you don't have any coverage, look into private insurance. If the policies offered seem too costly, look for cheaper ones that have a longer waiting period before the benefits kick in. If you buy a policy whose benefits don't begin until six months or a year after you become disabled, the premiums should be substantially lower. You can also cut costs by buying a policy that, instead of paying benefits for life, will provide benefits only through age 65, at which point Social Security retirement benefits should kick in.

Is there anybody who doesn't need disability insurance?

Ponder this: If you never worked again, would you suffer financially? If you are among the lucky few who are sufficiently wealthy that working is a matter of fun rather than necessity, you can probably do without disability insurance.

Umbrella Liability Insurance

Umbrella liability insurance provides protection in case you are sued. A policy providing $1 million of protection might cost as little as $100, which I consider a bargain in today's litigious society. But just as rich folks don't need disability or health insurance, so they can probably do without umbrella liability insurance. Once again, this is a risk they can afford to shoulder themselves.

If you are just out of school and you don't have much in the way of assets, you might also skip umbrella liability insurance, on the grounds that you are not worth suing because you don't have any assets. A good idea? I'm not so sure. If you are sued and you lose the lawsuit, you could find that a portion of your future wages are garnished.

Long-Term Care Insurance

Long-term care insurance, also sometimes called nursing-home insurance, is bought by those in their 50s and up to pay for nursing-home and for at-home care. There's a lot of debate about the merits of long-term care insurance and I am just not sure whether it's a good deal. Before buying, you should look long and hard at a host of policies and weigh the costs, benefits and alternatives. Part of the problem is that long-term care insurance just hasn't been around for that long, so it's difficult to know whether insurance companies are pricing policies far too high, far too low or just right. If they are pricing the policies too high, you will likely lose if you buy the policy. If they are pricing the policies too low, you have yourself a bargain—but it may not last long, because the insurance company could go bankrupt.

Long-term care policies get more expensive the later in life you first buy them, so often it pays to be early. On the other hand, if you have enough foresight to think about long-term care insurance when you are in your 50s, maybe you should just take the money that would have gone toward the policy and instead shovel it into an investment account. That way, if you get hit with nursing-home bills, you will be well-prepared.

LIFE INSURANCE IS A GOOD INVESTMENT

Life-insurance agents extol the virtues of cash-value life insurance with all the fervor of the evangelist. These policies will, they claim, provide money for your kid's college, protect your family in case you die, cut your income-tax bill, help you retire, bail you out in an emergency, save your heirs a fortune in estate taxes and help bring about world peace.

Okay, maybe not world peace. But agents do promise everything else, and more, if you purchase a cash-value life insurance policy. Can these policies really achieve all that's claimed for them? As they say on Wall Street, if it sounds like too much of a good thing, it probably is. Cash-value life insurance is, regrettably, no exception.

Where We Go Wrong

While there are bewildering variations, life-insurance policies fall into one of two broad camps, term insurance and cash-value life insurance. As insurance agents are quick to note, term insurance provides a death benefit and nothing more. You pay an annual premium, in return for which your heirs will get a fistful of money should you die within the next year. What if you don't die? Your premiums are gone and you have nothing to show for them.

Insurance agents will also point out that you often can't renew a term policy after age 70 and, even if you can, these policies grow increasingly costly. With some term insurance, you may need to take a medical exam periodically to keep the policy in force. Depending on the policy, the premiums you pay may adjust upward every year or they may only increase every five or 10 years. As you grow older and your chances of dying rise, term insurance can become prohibitively expensive.

All of these drawbacks are pounded home by an army of life-insurance agents, who will then contrast these flaws with the voluminous virtues of cash-value life insurance. Cash-value policies, which are sometimes also called "permanent" insurance, come in three varieties, whole life, universal life and variable life. The policies can be continued past age 70 and they are designed so that the annual premium shouldn't ever go up.

How do these policies manage this feat? Every year, part of your premium goes into an investment account, so that the policy gradually builds up cash value. With variable life, you can even control how the money is invested and you might opt to put part of your premiums in the stock market. Because more and more of a cash-value policy's promised death benefit comes to be represented by cash value, the pure insurance you buy each year gradually decreases. As a result, premiums on cash-value policies don't shoot up in the later years, as they do with term insurance.

Moreover, the cash value grows on a tax-deferred basis, so there are no income taxes to be paid each year. As the cash value climbs, you can borrow against the policy and you may be able to withdraw your accumulated premiums tax-free, which could prove helpful as you grapple with college costs. You can even cancel the policy, get back the cash value and then use it to help pay for retirement. But if you do keep the policy in force, it can provide substantial estate-tax savings. If you arrange for the policy to be owned by, say, an irrevocable life-insurance trust, rather than by yourself, the proceeds from the policy won't be subject to estate taxes.

Sound attractive? Life-insurance agents, who happen to earn fat commissions for selling these policies, certainly believe so. But there are, unfortunately, a few minor problems. Like the fact that cash-value policies are horribly expensive, that you have plenty of better ways to borrow, that you probably don't need life insurance past age 70, that you can get tax-deferred growth better and cheaper elsewhere and that you will probably never be rich enough to need the estate-tax savings. Just another oversold Wall Street contraption? You better believe it.

The New Rules

Insurance agents pitch cash-value life insurance as the universal panacea, solving every problem from taxes to college funding to retirement. But while these policies can indeed be used to achieve multiple goals, they don't achieve any of their objectives particularly well.

The principal reason to buy life insurance isn't to save on taxes or earn fat investment returns. Instead, the reason you buy life insurance is to protect your family in the event of your death. On that score, term insurance is a much better bet than cash-value life insurance because it's so much cheaper. A cash-value policy might cost eight times as much as a term-insurance policy with the same death benefit. The danger is, if you plunk for a cash-value policy, you might skimp on coverage because the premiums are so steep.

What about the escalating premiums on a term policy? What about the fact that you may not even be able to keep your term insurance in force beyond age 70? Big deal. By the time you reach 70, you probably won't have anybody who is financially dependent on you. Your kids will have left home and gotten established on their own. Meanwhile, your spouse shouldn't be dependent on your income anymore, because by age 70 the two of you together should

Terms of the Trade

If you go shopping for term insurance, you will likely be offered two types, annual renewable term and level premium term. With annual renewable term, the premium you pay rises each year, while a level premium policy allows you to pay the same amount each year for a stated period, typically five to 20 years. If you need term insurance for, say, the next 10 years and you can buy a level premium policy to cover this period, that would probably be your best bet. The problem is, if you need to keep the insurance in force beyond 10 years, you typically have to take another medical exam. If your health has deteriorated, your annual premium could soar.

As a result, if you are not sure how long you will need your term insurance, skip level premium policies and instead stick with annual renewable term insurance. Make sure the policy comes with guaranteed renewability. What's that? With these policies, once you have undergone the initial medical exam, you can continue the insurance without taking additional medical tests.

How do you find out more about term insurance? Here are a few places to start. To get quotes on term insurance from a host of companies, try one of the quote services, such as Insurance-Quote Services (800-972-1104), MasterQuote of America (800-337-5433), QuickQuote Insurance Agency (800-867-2404), Quotesmith Corporation (800-431-1147), SelectQuote Insurance Services (800-343-1985) and TermQuote (800-444-8376). Alternatively, if you are an Internet user, visit InstantQuote Online Insurance Services (http://www.instantquote.com), InsuranceQuote (http://www.iquote.com), MasterQuote (http://masterquote.com), QuickQuote (http://quickquote.com), Quotesmith (http://quotesmith.com) and TermQuote (http://www.rcinet.com/~termquote). You may also be able to get cheap term insurance through your employer or through professional associations that you are a member of. If that route doesn't pan out, try USAA Life Insurance Co. (800-531-8000), a top-rated insurer that offers term insurance at reasonable rates.

have accumulated a substantial nest egg to carry you through retirement. Very few people really need "permanent" insurance. Most folks are much better off buying cheap term insurance, which, after the initial medical exam, can be kept in force for as long as the policy is needed without taking any more medical tests.

Of course, the reason permanent insurance is so expensive is that you are building up cash value. But just as cash-value life insurance is a costly way to protect your family, it's also an expensive way to build an investment account. If you buy a cash-value policy through an insurance agent, you will lose most of your first year's premium to the agent's commission. As a result, if you cancel the policy in the first few years—as all too many consumers do—you will receive back only a tiny fraction of the premiums you paid.

Those who keep at it will do better. The initial hit from the agent's commission will fade and the cash value will start to build on a tax-deferred basis. But there are many other ways to get tax-deferred growth. You can put the money in an individual retirement account. You can stuff savings into your employer's 401(k) or 403(b) plan. These retirement accounts typically aren't burdened by all the commissions and administrative overhead of a cash-value policy, so your money will grow that much more rapidly. What about the borrowing privileges that come with cash-value policies? Who cares. You could also borrow from your 401(k) or 403(b) plan or tap the equity in your home.

All right, so there are cheaper ways to buy insurance and better ways to get investment growth. But what about the estate-tax savings? This is an undoubted advantage. But buying life insurance for estate-tax purposes only makes sense if you and your spouse expect to leave more than $1.2 million to your heirs. For those who are single, estate taxes become an issue if you bequeath more than $600,000. These thresholds will gradually increase over the next decade, as a result of the 1997 tax bill. What if your estate isn't likely to top those lofty thresholds? You don't need life insurance for estate-tax purposes.

For most folks, there just isn't much value in cash-value life insurance. So do yourself a favor. Hang on to your cash.

INVEST IN YOUR KID'S NAME

Maybe there's no such thing as a bad tax break. But putting money in your kid's name comes pretty close.

Yet everybody says you should do it. Mutual-fund companies exhort shareholders to open custodial accounts for their children. Many accountants, brokers and financial planners tout the benefits. Grandparents love the idea of putting money in their new grandchild's name. It's hardly surprising that lots of parents—my wife and I included—have ended up shoveling dollars into custodial accounts. After all, with the price tag on four years at some private colleges now topping $100,000, you need all the help you can get.

But is it such a good idea to put money in a kid's name? The brutal reality is, it's a tax ploy without much tax benefit—but with a lot of associated headaches.

Where We Go Wrong

Why shouldn't you put money in a child's name? Here are four good reasons:

■ You won't save much in taxes.

Thanks to the 1986 tax act, Uncle Sam isn't exactly generous if you open custodial accounts for children who are under age 14. If your kids are under 14 and you invest in their names, the first $650 of investment earnings is tax-free and the next $650 is taxed at a maximum rate of 15 percent. Above $1,300, all investment gains are taxed at the parents' rate. These earnings thresholds are boosted every few years to reflect inflation.

Once a child turns 14, the tax man is more generous. The first $650 of investment earnings is tax-free. Thereafter, all gains are taxed at the child's rate, which will usually be 15 percent. Unfortunately, however, by the time kids reach age 14, they are only four or five years away from college, so it's a little late to start a long-term investment program aimed at paying for Princeton.

■ You lose control.

If you are going to invest in your kids' names and you are dealing with relatively modest sums, it's just not worth paying an attorney to set up a trust. So instead, you will probably take the low-budget route favored by most parents, which is to open custodial accounts under your state's Uniform Gifts to Minors Act or Uniform Transfers to Minors Act. With UGMA and UTMA accounts, children get control of the money when they reach the age of majority, usually 18 or 21, depending on the state.

That $25,000 college fund, which you lovingly built by socking away $50 or $100 at a time, might have been intended to cover the first year at an Ivy League college. But because you surrender control when your child turns 18 or 21, it could end up going toward a little red sports car. Or a trip around the world. Or a drug habit that's painful even to contemplate. As you cradle your newborn, it's hard to imagine any of these things could happen. But unfortunately, sometimes they do.

If the age of majority in your state is 21, you should be safe, because by the time your children reach that age, their custodial accounts will likely have been emptied to pay for the first few years of college. But if your state's age of majority is 18, you could have a problem, because the kids will get their hands on the money before a single dime has gone toward tuition.

An additional word of warning. If you are the person funding a custodial account, you may want to ask somebody else to be custodian. How come? If you die before your children reach the age of majority and you had both funded the custodial accounts and also named yourself as the custodian, the accounts are included in your estate and could be subject to estate taxes.

■ You hurt your kids' chances of financial aid.

The financial-aid system is an abomination desperately in need of reform, not least because the system penalizes parents who save for college by putting money in their children's names. Under the federal financial-aid formula, kids are expected to put 35 percent of their savings toward each year's college expenses. Meanwhile, parents only have to pony up a maximum of 5.65 percent of assets held in their own names. Individual colleges, when doling out the aid they control, also expect kids to cough up a disproportionate amount of their savings.

The result is that, if you put a lot of money in your children's custodial accounts, you could wreck your chances of getting financial aid. You may, of course, think that your children couldn't possibly qualify for aid. This is a tough call to make, however, because the aid formulas used are so complicated. If your family income is $70,000 or $80,000, you probably won't get much in the way of grants and loans, unless your children attend top-priced colleges or you have two or more kids in college at the same time. But stories abound of families with six-figure incomes getting impressive amounts of financial aid.

Even if you think your chances of aid are currently slim, how can you be sure that you will always be earning such a lofty salary? If your finances take a turn for the worse, because you lose your job or your career gets sidetracked by illness, you may suddenly find that your family is eligible for aid. At that point, all those dollars that you dutifully stashed in custodial accounts will come back to haunt you.

You may feel it's unethical to arrange your finances to improve your chances of aid. You're not alone. Lots of folks don't like the idea of "financial-aid planning," because they feel they are somehow gaming the system and will end up receiving grant money that would have gone to others. But in all likelihood, if your children are not considered that financially needy, most of the aid they receive will take the form of low-interest loans rather than grants. These loans can ease the financial burden of attending college, turning it into a far more pleasurable experience for both you and your children. Given what's at stake, do you really want to deny yourself and your kids all possibility of financial assistance?

■ You limit your investment options.

If you invest in your children's names, it's tough to know how to invest the money. If your children are at least six or seven years from college, clearly you want to have some of their college money in stocks and clearly you want to be well-diversified, which means stock-mutual funds are your best bet. But which funds? It's not an easy decision. Ideally, you would like to build a global stock portfolio, with at least a blue-chip stock fund, a small-company stock fund and a foreign-stock fund. You could easily do that if you are holding your kids' college savings in your own name and thus mixing the money with your retirement, emergency and other savings.

But if you invest in your children's names, the sums involved will be relatively small, so building a full-blown fund portfolio will probably seem like more trouble than it's worth. As an alternative, I have often suggested that folks use one of the lifecycle funds, which offer a well-diversified portfolio in a single mutual fund. But these aren't an ideal choice. Why not? When it comes time to cash out your children's college money, U.S. stocks may be riding high, but foreign stocks could be in a slump. As a result, you might want to sell the U.S. stocks first, while you wait for the foreign stocks to recover. But with a lifecycle fund, you can't do that. When you sell fund shares, you will be cashing out of everything, large stocks, small stocks and foreign stocks.

The New Rules

Investing in your children's names involves tricky issues of control, financial aid and investment strategy. On the other hand, there is the chance to get a modest tax break, and that's tough to resist. What should you do? A lot depends on your family's situation. Here are three strategies, for those who expect financial aid, for those who don't expect aid and are currently in the 15 percent tax bracket and for those who don't expect aid and are in the 28 percent or above tax bracket:

■ If you expect financial aid, don't put any money in your children's names.

Instead, if you want to sock away money for college, keep the investments in your own name. This money will still be counted against you when applying for aid, but the accounting isn't nearly so punitive. If you are a more conservative investor, also consider making extra-principal payments on your mortgage, with a view to paying off your mortgage by the time your children enter college. That will free up money each month that can then be put toward college expenses. Even if you don't get your mortgage paid off in time, you will still build up home equity, which you can then borrow against to help with tuition costs. For those who expect financial aid, paying down your mortgage can be a particularly good strategy. Unlike regular savings, your home equity doesn't count against you under the federal financial-aid formula. Many colleges, however, consider home equity when parceling out their own aid.

Alternatively, consider socking away college savings in an individual retirement account or one of the new education IRAs. Just as home equity isn't considered under the federal financial-aid formula, retirement-account assets also don't currently count against you. But this may change. Moreover, retirement money is looked at by some colleges when making decisions about the aid they control.

Nonetheless, retirement accounts are an intriguing option for college savers, thanks to the 1997 tax bill. The bill not only allows parents to make penalty-free withdrawals from their IRAs to pay college expenses, it also created a new education IRA. Couples with earnings below $150,000 can put $500 a year into an education IRA for each of their children. The money grows tax-deferred until its withdrawn, at which point there are no taxes owed as long as the money is put toward education expenses.

The education IRA strikes me as a good deal, as does the chance to tap your retirement IRAs for college expenses. But there is a catch. If you withdraw money from these accounts to pay for college, it will boost your income and thus may hurt your children's aid eligibility. Try to avoid tapping these accounts until after you have completed your final financial-aid application. That means these accounts are best used to pay for your child's senior year at college.

More conservative investors might also consider EE savings bonds. When you sell these bonds, the interest can be tax-free. But to get the tax break, the proceeds from selling the bonds must be used to pay for eligible educational expenses, the bonds must be owned by the parents and not the kids, and you must be below certain income thresholds when you cash in the bonds. In addition, for some inexplicable reason, parents can only claim the tax break if they were at least 24 years old when they purchased the bonds.

■ If you don't expect financial aid and you are currently in the 15 percent tax bracket, put up to $8,000 in a custodial account for each child.

Of course, if you are still in the 15 percent bracket when your kids apply for college, you should be eligible for a healthy amount of grants and loans, unless you have substantial assets. But maybe you are currently on a fairly low salary but you expect much higher earnings down the road, which will make your family ineligible for aid. What to do? Until you get into a higher tax bracket, save no more than $8,000 in each kid's name.

Why $8,000? If you invest that much money in your son's name and he earns 8 percent in realized investment gains each year, he will have annual gains of close to $650, which is the amount that he can earn tax-free. Hitting this $650 is trickier than you might imagine. Most parents would be well-advised to buy stock-mutual funds for their kid's college savings. But the annual fund distributions—especially the capital-gains distributions—fluctuate sharply from year to year, so that some years your son could earn substantially more than $650 and some years he may receive far less.

If your son earns anything more than $650, the money will be taxed at a maximum rate of 15 percent, which is the same as the rate you are taxed at. Thus, if you put a lot more than $8,000 in your son's name and he ends up receiving more than $650 in realized investment gains each year, you won't get any tax benefit, but you will be sacrificing control and you will have to start filing a tax return on your son's behalf. You could also be messing up your chances of financial aid, should you turn out to be eligible.

What if you want to sock away more than $8,000 for college? Consider keeping the money in your name. You could use these dollars to pay down your mortgage or you could stash the money in a regular taxable account, an IRA or an education IRA.

■ If you don't expect financial aid and you are currently in the 28 percent tax bracket or above, put up to $16,000 in a custodial account for each child under age 14.

With $16,000 in your 8-year-old daughter's name, she will be earning close to $1,300 a year, presuming that her investments kick off a realized investment gain of 8 percent each year. The first $650 is tax-free and the next $650 is taxed at a maximum rate of 15 percent. Once your daughter starts earning above $1,300 a year, there's no point in putting further dollars in her name, because all investment gains above $1,300 will be taxed at your rate anyway. Moreover, if your daughter is under 14 and she does earn more than $1,300 in investment income, you have to file the horribly complicated Internal Revenue Service Form 8615 along with your kid's tax return.

Everything changes once your daughter reaches age 14. At that point, she can earn a lot more than $1,300 and still get taxed at 15 percent. But before you start shoveling money into an account in her name, make sure that she seems responsible and double-check that you have no chance of financial aid. Also, make sure that you really are in the 28 percent tax bracket or above.

If it makes sense to invest a lot more money in your daughter's name, consider making a gift to her of shares you own that have appreciated greatly in value. She can then sell the shares and pay taxes on the appreciation at her tax rate. By law, both you and your spouse can make gifts of up to $10,000 a year to anybody else and there's no limit on the number of $10,000 gifts you can make. That means that every year you and your spouse could together give up to $20,000 worth of stock to each of your children.

If you give more than $10,000 to anybody else in any one year, you trigger the gift tax. This particular tax is thrown in to dissuade you from giving away all your money to your kids before you die, thereby avoiding estate taxes. But there's an exception to this, which is worth mentioning to well-heeled grandparents. If you pay educational expenses for somebody else, this money isn't counted toward the $10,000 annual gift-tax exclusion. But to avoid the gift tax, you have to pay the money directly to the educational institution involved, so make sure the grandparents send the check to Harvard and not to you.

MAX OUT YOUR IRA
EVERY YEAR

It's the 11th commandment of personal finance. It's one of the great acts of high financial rectitude. It's what mother would have wanted you to do.

We are, of course, talking about stuffing money into individual retirement accounts, variable annuities and other tax-sheltered savings vehicles. True, your contribution may not be tax-deductible. But you still get the tax-deferred growth, so that you don't have to pay taxes on any investment gains until the money is withdrawn. Maybe more important, you put the money out of reach, which means you are less likely to spend it and more likely to have a bigger nest egg come retirement.

What could possibly be wrong with that, you cry? As it happens, I was hoping you would ask that question.

Where We Go Wrong

Individual retirement accounts and other tax-sheltered savings vehicles bring with them a fistful of headaches. Here are four major drawbacks:

■ Your money is locked up.

You may be able to take out a loan from your employer's retirement plan. But you can't borrow from an IRA or a variable annuity and it's tricky to withdraw money before age 59½ without getting hit with a 10 percent tax penalty. Result? Unless you are in your 50s, at which point it may be worth pulling out money from your IRA and variable annuity using "substantially equal periodic payments" (see Myth No. 16), you really can't touch these investments before retirement.

That may seem attractive if you are an ill-disciplined investor who finds it tough to save. But the attraction may lose some of its luster if you get laid off, or you fall ill, or you are faced with a major home repair. Suddenly, you need a lot of money, but you discover that most of your investments are sitting in your IRA and other tax-sheltered savings plans. Unless you are allowed to take out a loan against your 401(k) or 403(b) plan, the cost of getting to this money can be horrendous, thanks to income taxes and the 10 percent tax penalty.

What to do? Take a look at how your investments are divvied up between retirement and regular taxable accounts. You may find that you have substantial amounts of money in your IRA, variable annuity and 401(k) or 403(b) plan and precious little in your taxable accounts. If that's the case, maybe you should skip your retirement-account contributions for the next few years, especially if these contributions aren't tax-deductible. Instead, put these dollars in a regular taxable account, where the money will be easily accessible if you get hit with an emergency.

■ You are turning capital gains into income.

If you are saving for retirement or any other long-term investment goal, you should be investing in stocks. With stocks, most of the gain takes the form of capital appreciation, which is a big plus. Why? Your income may be taxed at 28 percent, 31 percent or more, but your long-term capital gains are taxed at no more than 20 percent. Unfortunately, however, with a variable annuity or a retirement account—whether it's an IRA, a 401(k) plan or a 403(b) plan—the tax advantage enjoyed by capital gains gets annihilated. When you pull money out of these accounts, all taxable gains are taxed as ordinary income, even if most of the gains came from capital appreciation.

■ You are setting yourself up for tax hassles.

High-income earners are told constantly by experts to fund their IRAs, even if the contributions aren't tax-deductible and even if they don't qualify for the Roth IRA. But if you make nondeductible contributions to a regular IRA, you are guaranteeing yourself at least one day of aggravation every year throughout retirement. When you pull these nondeductible contributions out of your IRA, you don't have to pay income tax on them, which seems like a plus, until you see what's involved. If the Internal Revenue Service had an ounce of kindness and common sense, it would allow you to pull these nondeductible contributions out of your retirement account as soon as you retire, thereby eliminating all hassles. Instead, the IRS, in its infinite wisdom, insists that you presume that every dollar withdrawn from your retirement account is a mix of taxable and nontaxable money. My advice? Take two aspirin and see an accountant in the morning.

■ Even death offers no escape from the tax man.

Your spouse can inherit your variable annuity, IRA and other retirement accounts without too many hassles. But if you leave these accounts to anybody else, things can get pretty messy. Even if your total estate is small and your retirement accounts are modest, all the income taxes owed on your retirement accounts still have to be paid after your death and the money in the account may have to be pulled out fairly quickly.

You can try to sidestep these rules, but it's horribly complicated. If you name, say, a child as the primary beneficiary of your retirement accounts by shortly after age 70½, it's possible to figure minimum withdrawals over the joint life expectancy of you and the child. After you die, the child inherits the account and can then figure minimum distributions over his or her own life expectancy, thus stringing out the withdrawals—and the related income-tax payments—for years and years. While this strategy is appealing, not many folks use it, because they need the money to fund their own retirement or because, at age 70½, they are still not sure whether their spouse will need their retirement-account money and thus they are reluctant to name a child as the primary beneficiary.

Because retirement accounts are such a mess to bequeath, you might want to leave your retirement accounts to charity, thus killing the problem with kindness. Meanwhile, to keep the kids from grousing, leave them your other assets. Unlike retirement accounts, these other assets—such as your house and investments held in regular taxable accounts—enjoy "stepped-up basis," which means your children inherit these items at their current market value and thus there are no income taxes or capital-gains taxes owed. Estate taxes, however, will still have to be paid, presuming you die with substantial assets.

Two additional thoughts. First, if you made nondeductible contributions to your IRA, make sure your heirs know about them, so that they don't inadvertently pay income taxes on these contributions. Second, be aware that your retirement-account assets will probably go to the beneficiaries you named on the retirement-account registration forms, even if you named different beneficiaries in your will. Indeed, upon your death, your retirement accounts usually go straight to the beneficiary named on the accounts, rather than going through the legal review known as probate, as happens with many other assets.

The New Rules

Maybe you are starting to think that tax-sheltered savings accounts aren't all they are cracked up to be. Not so. These accounts are usually a good deal—but not always.

Here's the way I look at it. If you can make tax-deductible contributions to your employer's retirement-savings plan and get a matching contribution from your company, it's undoubtedly the best investment deal available, and you should shovel every penny legally possible into the account. If you can make tax-deductible contributions to an IRA or to your employer's plan, it's also worth doing, even if there is no matching contribution. After all, you still get the up-front tax deduction and the tax-deferred growth. Similarly, if you qualify for the Roth IRA, you should take advantage if you can.

When it comes to making nondeductible contributions to an employer's plan, I am on the fence. The good news is, when you leave your employer, you can get these contributions returned to you, free of income taxes and tax penalties. Thus, you avoid the messy tax accounting that comes with nondeductible IRA contributions, you get tax-deferred growth and you have access to the money before age 59½. The downside is, to get hold of the money without triggering taxes and penalties, you typically have to quit your job. What if you need the dollars before you leave your employer? You're stuck.

But my real beef is with variable annuities and nondeductible IRA contributions. Sure, with an IRA, you get tax-deferred growth. But you also lock up the money, set yourself up for tax hassles and turn capital gains into income. As an alternative, some brokers, financial planners and insurance agents advocate variable annuities. Variable annuities are ostensibly an insurance product, but they are really just another way to buy investments on a tax-deferred basis. Indeed, the rules for variable annuities are quite similar to those that govern retirement accounts. But with a variable annuity, you can invest an unlimited amount each year. The problem is, variable annuities suffer all the other problems of retirement accounts, plus they are often horribly expensive, so it's tough to earn decent investment returns.

If you have more than enough money sitting in taxable accounts, go ahead and make nondeductible IRA contributions and stuff money into variable annuities. But if your taxable account is on the thin side, ignore all the experts telling you to fund your nondeductible IRA and buy variable annuities. Instead, stick the money into a taxable account. That way, you will avoid a lot of tax hassles and you will ensure easy access to your money, which means you will be better prepared should an emergency strike.

Give the Gift of Time

Variable annuities are a mediocre investment. Consider buying them for your kids.

What gives? Variable annuities have a lot of drawbacks, not least of which are the hefty costs involved. But given tax-deferred growth over a long enough period, even this disadvantage can be overcome. Which is where your kids come in.

Buying a variable annuity for a child has two big advantages. First, unlike a retirement account, a variable annuity doesn't require that you have any earned income in order to buy one, so it's possible to purchase one for your unemployed toddler. Second, when you buy a variable annuity, you are buying the chance to invest in the mutual-fund subaccounts. Some of these subaccounts will invest in stocks, thus giving you the chance to get stock-market compounding on a grand scale.

Suppose you put $5,000 into a variable annuity for your three-year-old son. You buy one of the subaccounts that invests in stocks and the account goes on to earn 9 percent a year. By the time your child retires at age 65, his variable annuity is valued at over $1 million. Thanks to inflation of, say, 3 percent a year, that $1 million will only be worth $167,000 in today's dollars. But I'm sure your kid won't complain too loudly.

Buying a variable annuity for a child has a couple of additional benefits. Because of the 10 percent penalty on early withdrawals, your child will be deterred from tapping the account before age 59½. Moreover, while money placed in your kid's name usually hurts your family's chances of financial aid, not many colleges pay attention to variable annuities. This may change, however.

Interested? My advice: Stick with one of the lower-cost annuities. Check out the offerings from Fidelity Investments (800-634-9361), Janus Funds (800-504-4440), T. Rowe Price Associates (800-469-6587), Charles Schwab Corporation (800-838-0650), Scudder Funds (800-242-4402), USAA Life Insurance Co. (800-531-4265) and Vanguard Group (800-462-2391).

You will, however, have to pay tax each year on any invest-ment gains kicked off by your taxable accounts. But you can skirt this problem. If you are a conservative investor and you are in the 28 percent tax bracket or above, consider municipal bonds or mu-nicipal-bond funds, which will kick off interest that's exempt from federal taxes. This interest will also be exempt from state and local taxes, if you buy bonds from your own state.

More aggressive investors can also hold down their tax bill by buying and holding stocks. You will have to pay income taxes on the dividends you receive each year. But the capital-gains taxes on any price appreciation don't have to be paid until the stocks are sold. Buying and holding stocks is, of course, what index funds do. These mutual funds, which simply purchase the stocks that constitute an index in an effort to match the index's perfor-mance, usually make only modest capital-gains distributions each year, so they are a great choice for your taxable account. Instead of stuffing money into a nondeductible IRA or a variable annuity, buy a global portfolio of index funds in your taxable account. Like an IRA, these index funds also give you tax-deferred growth—but without all the tax hassles.

MYTH NO.

ONE DAY, KIDS, ALL OF THIS WILL BE YOURS

Many profligate baby boomers are apparently waiting for their parents to die, so that they can then retire on the much-anticipated inheritance. Ghoulish? Certainly. Pathetic? I think so. Unlikely to happen? You got it.

The fact is, most retirees won't leave heaps of money to their kids or their favorite charity. Sure, by one estimate, $5 trillion will be transferred from one generation to the next over the coming 20 years. Some put the number even higher. But the bulk of this money will pass among the wealthiest families. Most retirees will leave little behind. They will find they need virtually every penny saved to pay for a retirement that might last 20 or 25 years. Think of the pitfalls. These folks could live longer than they planned for. They might spend years in a nursing home they never made provision for. They may incur huge unreimbursed medical expenses before they die. They could lose a fistful of money to estate taxes.

But if you are determined to leave a bundle to your kids or to charity, you can probably do it. It's not going to happen, however, if you don't think ahead, unpleasant as that may be. Death is no different from any other aspect of personal finance. You still have to plan. True, you don't know when or how you are going to die. But there's still a lot you can do. You can make sure you save enough money to carry you through a long retirement. You can ensure you have adequate medical coverage, especially to cover hospitalization. You can put aside money to cover nursing-home costs or take out long-term care insurance. And, as you will discover below, you can take steps to make sure your affairs are well-organized and to minimize the hit from estate taxes. You can also spell out your wishes concerning life-prolonging medical procedures.

Where We Go Wrong

Don't get me wrong. I am not saying that your well-laid plans won't go awry. It's quite possible that, even if you have every intention of leaving heaps of money to your kids, you will live far longer than you ever imagined or saved for. The bottom line? You may want to leave your kids a bundle. But your children would be foolish to expect it.

I am also not saying you should scrimp and save so that your kids inherit a small fortune. Maybe, instead, you want to spend it all, traveling the world and having the time of your life. If that is what you choose to do with your hard-earned savings, I think it's admirable.

The big mistake, I believe, is not making any choices at all. In an inevitably unsuccessful act of denial, many folks choose to ignore their own mortality. Their kids, meanwhile, aren't likely to broach the subject. After all, they don't want to appear greedy or morbid. So why not forget the whole unpleasant topic? You may not live to regret this decision. But everybody around you almost certainly will. Here are just some of the possible consequences of your inaction:

■ You could be the subject of life-prolonging medical procedures, even though there's no chance you could recover and enjoy a meaningful existence.

■ Your spouse and kids may not be able to locate all your assets, including investment accounts, valuables you have hidden around the house and items you have stashed in a safe-deposit box.

■ You could end up leaving property to the wrong person, because you died without a will or because your assets weren't properly titled.

■ Your life insurance might be subject to estate taxes, when an easy fix could save you thousands of dollars.

■ If you are married, your family could end up forking over an extra $235,000 in estate taxes because you failed to take advantage of a simple estate-planning maneuver.

■ Your spouse and kids could blow $10,000 on an elaborate funeral, when you might prefer a simple $1,000 cremation.

Sound dire? Let's face it, it's enough to make you turn over in your fancy new mausoleum.

The New Rules

Like so many personal-finance topics, estate planning is a lot less complicated than it seems. Admittedly, you still need a good attorney to draw up a will and the other legal documents you require. But unless you have a huge estate, the actual strategies involved are fairly easy to understand. Here are seven key components of any decent estate plan.

Bypassing the Tax Man

If you leave everything to your spouse, no estate taxes are due. You can also leave a total of up to $600,000 to everybody else and avoid estate taxes. As part of the 1997 tax bill, this threshold rises to $625,000 in 1998, $650,000 in 1999 and so on, until it hits $1 million in 2006. Once bequests top $600,000, estate taxes kick in, starting at 37 percent and rising rapidly from there. Everybody gets this $600,000 lifetime federal estate-tax exemption, also known as the "unified credit." But lots of married folks fail to use it.

How come? On their death, they leave everything to their spouse, effectively wasting their $600,000 estate-tax exemption. If you and your spouse have total assets of less than $600,000, including your house and all your investment accounts combined, this is the right thing to do. What if you have more than $600,000? You may want to ensure that both you and your spouse take advantage of the $600,000 federal estate-tax exemption. To do this, ask your attorney about using a bypass trust, also known as a unified credit-shelter trust.

With a bypass trust, on the death of the first spouse, up to $600,000 goes into a trust with the money earmarked for, say, the kids, but with assets still available to the surviving spouse. This uses the first spouse's estate-tax exemption. On the death of the second spouse, another $600,000 will avoid estate taxes, so that a total of $1.2 million passes to the kids tax-free. By making sure both spouses use the $600,000 exemption, you save $235,000 in estate taxes.

Simple, right? Here's one complication. Unless you live in a community property state, such as California or Texas, it's tough to fund a bypass trust with assets that are owned jointly with right of survivorship. Most couples title their homes and their investment accounts this way, because it seems like the married thing to do. But when the first spouse dies, these jointly owned assets automatically pass to the surviving spouse, which means they can't go into a bypass trust. A good attorney can get around this problem through the use of a disclaimer clause. But it's messy. To avoid the problem, consider holding at least some assets separately, even if you and your spouse are young and you don't yet have anything like $600,000 in assets. That way, if you do later accumulate substantial assets, you will be well-placed to fund a bypass trust.

Gifts That Keep On Giving

You can also avoid estate taxes by gradually giving away money to your kids and other beneficiaries. By law, each year you can give up to $10,000 to anybody else—kids, cousins, the mailman, whomever—without worrying about the gift tax. That means that, if you and your spouse have three children, you can together give each of your kids $20,000 a year, for a total of $60,000. If you give more than $10,000 in any one year, the excess will be counted against your $600,000 exemption, so that less money can pass tax-free upon your death.

There are two ways to sidestep this $10,000 limit. If you help somebody with either medical costs or educational expenses, this money isn't counted against the annual $10,000 gift-tax exclusion. Grandparents, for instance, might pay college costs for a grandchild, which would have the pleasant side-effect of reducing the size of their estates. But to avoid triggering the gift tax, make sure the money is paid directly to the medical provider or educational institution concerned.

Your Money or Your Life Insurance

If you own a life insurance policy that, say, names your children as the beneficiaries, the proceeds of the policy are included in your estate and subject to taxes. But if somebody else owns an insurance policy on your life, no estate tax is owed when you die.

What should you do if you have already purchased a policy on your own life? If you have a substantial estate, it may be worth assigning the policy to an irrevocable life-insurance trust, with, say, your children named as the beneficiaries of the trust. As long as you don't die within three years of transferring the policy, no estate taxes will have to be paid on the insurance proceeds. Alternatively, if you are healthy, you could take out new insurance policies and arrange for these policies to be purchased either directly by your children or by an irrevocable life-insurance trust.

Of course, life insurance can be horribly expensive, especially if you purchase cash-value life insurance or you buy insurance when you are older. It can, nonetheless, be worth it, because it provides a way of transferring assets to the next generation tax-free. But because of the expenses involved, you should consider life insurance for estate-tax purposes only after you have exhausted other options, such as using a bypass trust and gifting assets to your children.

Naming Names

Your assets will usually go to whomever you specified in your will. But there are some big exceptions. The proceeds from your life insurance go to the beneficiary you listed with the insurance company. Property that's owned jointly with right of survivorship automatically goes to the survivor. A retirement account goes to the person you named as the beneficiary on the account-registration form. What if you named Uncle Joey as your retirement account's beneficiary, but later decided in your will that you want everything to go to Cousin Doris? Unless you changed the beneficiary listed on the retirement account, Uncle Joey gets the money.

Indeed, retirement accounts, insurance policies and jointly owned property pass directly to the new owner and don't even go through the legal review known as probate. In probate, your will is reviewed, your assets toted up, creditors and state inheritance taxes paid and the assets then distributed. Lots of folks assume that, just because retirement accounts, insurance policies and jointly owned assets usually avoid probate, they also avoid estate taxes. Not true. What can happen, however, is that the folks who inherit your retirement account, insurance proceeds or jointly owned property may fail to pay their fair share of the estate taxes. If, for instance, you own a mutual fund jointly with your son, he may receive the account free of estate taxes on your death. But most or all of the account's value will be assessed against your $600,000 estate-tax exemption. Result? Your son avoids estate taxes on this one asset, which means all your other beneficiaries will end up paying a disproportionate amount of estate taxes. You may be able to get around this problem by having your lawyer insert a clause in your will stating that all beneficiaries should pay their prorated share of the estate taxes.

Completing the Paper Chase

In addition to a will, a bypass trust and an irrevocable life-insurance trust, also consider drawing up a durable power of attorney, a health-care power of attorney, a living will and a living trust. A durable power of attorney allows somebody else to complete financial transactions for you, if you become incapacitated. A health-care power of attorney appoints somebody to make medical decisions on your behalf, if you are unable to do so yourself. A living will specifies your wishes concerning life-prolonging medical procedures. Finally, you can establish a revocable living trust to hold your assets, thereby avoiding probate, which can be costly and slow and can involve publicity.

Organize Thyself

Yes, I know, this doesn't seem like an "estate-planning technique." But it could turn out to be at least as critical as everything else you do. Draw up a letter of instructions, which can act as a road map for your estate. Specify who should receive your personal belongings. Attach a list of all your assets and financial accounts, including real estate, bank accounts, mutual funds, stocks, bonds, brokerage accounts, credit cards and insurance policies. Note where account statements, stock certificates, property deeds, birth certificates, marriage certificates and old tax returns can be found. List the names of your accountant, broker, financial planner, insurance agent and lawyer.

In the letter of instructions, also detail what sort of funeral you want. Don't forget to mention if you have already bought a burial plot or prepaid your funeral. If you have a safe-deposit box, add that to the list. You may want to keep a copy of your funeral instructions, will and letter of instructions in your safe-deposit box. But also keep other copies elsewhere, where family members know to find them.

The Talking Cure

If you draw up a living will because you want a dignified death, it's not going to help if nobody knows the document exists. If your kids can't expect to inherit anything, it's only fair that you tell them. If you have written a detailed letter of instructions, it's utterly useless unless family members know where to find it. Estate planning involves death and money, two of the big taboos. Uncomfortable talking about these topics? Death is a chance to show your love and concern for your family, and for them to reciprocate. You might as well seize the opportunity. It's the last chance you are going to get.

THE NEW RULES FOR FINANCIAL SUCCESS

Ignore your friends, neighbors and colleagues. Stop listening to your parents. Don't pay any attention to the experts. Forget the conventional wisdom. Ditch the myths. It's time to rethink your every investment strategy. What should you be doing with your hard-earned cash? For those who nodded off during some of the earlier chapters, here's the *Reader's Digest* version:

■ You can't have it all, which means you have to make choices and make plans, so that you realize those goals that are important to you.

■ Forget about traditional company pensions and don't bank on generous Social Security benefits. If you want to retire in comfort, you have to save diligently, invest intelligently and make full use of your employer's retirement-savings plan.

■ If you are a long-term investor, your greatest enemies are inflation and taxes, not short-term market gyrations. To combat those two threats, your best bet is to invest heavily in stocks.

■ If you want top-notch investment returns, don't focus on finding high-flying stocks, or picking stellar mutual funds, or guessing the direction of the market. The biggest influence on your portfolio's return is how you divvy up your money among stocks, bonds and cash investments. The more you shovel into stocks, the higher your long-run returns.

■ Because of the punishing impact of mutual-fund expenses, brokerage commissions and other investment costs, you aren't likely to beat the market. What to do? Don't fret over finding investments that will outpace the stock-market averages. Instead, get an edge on other investors by holding down your investment costs.

■ As you map out your savings strategy for retirement or your kid's college education, be reasonable about your likely returns, so that you don't mistakenly save too little. Even if you are heavily invested in stocks, your portfolio isn't likely to make 10 percent a year over the long haul.

■ Avoid stock funds that aren't a useful addition to a low-cost, well-diversified portfolio. In particular, skip those funds that charge sales commissions or have high annual expenses. Also steer clear of global funds, regional funds, sector funds, balanced funds and most asset-allocation funds.

■ If you want stock funds that will generate dazzling results, look for small funds run by managers who have performed consistently well over long periods compared to other managers who use a similar investment style. Then keep your fingers crossed.

■ Index funds—which simply mimic the performance of the market averages—should be the top choice of rational investors who want to earn decent returns while outpacing most other stock-market investors.

■ Bank money-market accounts, certificates of deposit and savings accounts are anything but safe, because their lowly yields offer scant protection against inflation and taxes. Instead, if you want to hold cash investments, look to money-market mutual funds.

■ Despite their rich yields, most bonds and bond funds are a rotten investment because they are volatile, tax-inefficient, difficult to trade, provide little defense against inflation and are a poor diversifier for stocks.

■ Don't bother with hard assets. They are expensive to own, difficult to trade and poor performing, and they don't offer reliable portfolio protection to stock-market investors.

■ The traditional balanced portfolio, with its mix of blue-chip stocks and longer-term bonds, no longer works, because both halves of the portfolio are now driven by interest rates. As an alternative, look to combine stocks with zero-coupon bonds, money-market funds, inflation-indexed bonds and short-term taxable or municipal-bond funds.

■ If you are willing to make your own investment decisions, you no longer need a full-service broker, thanks to the emergence of no-load mutual funds, no-load stocks and discount brokers. And if you do need advice, there are plenty of options, including not only full-service brokers, but also a slew of fee-based financial planners.

■ A popular rule of thumb states that, as an emergency reserve, you should keep six months of living expenses stashed in conservative investments. But for most folks, I believe this is far too much. Consider either keeping a smaller cash hoard, equal to maybe three months' living expenses, or shooting for the large amount, but investing much of the money in stocks.

■ In case disaster strikes, make sure you can borrow easily, by tapping margin accounts, employer retirement plans, home equity, cash-value life insurance and credit cards.

■ If you want to build up a lot of home equity quickly, don't buy the biggest house possible. Instead, buy a smaller house and then either take out a shorter mortgage or make extra-mortgage payments.

■ Mortgage interest may be tax-deductible. But it's still costing you a lot more than it's costing Uncle Sam. Making extra-mortgage payments—so that you cut down your mortgage-interest costs—can be a good investment if you would otherwise put the money in bonds or cash investments.

■ Home improvements are a guaranteed money loser. Build a deck, if that's what you really want. But don't expect to recoup the deck's cost when you sell your home.

■ Trading up to a larger house is a sure-fire way to lose a

fistful of money in real-estate transaction costs. It's only worth buying a bigger house if you really want the extra space.

■ The odds are, when you buy insurance, the money spent is money down the drain. Purchase policies that provide broad protection against truly catastrophic events. Ignore the rest.

■ Cash-value life insurance usually isn't a good investment. It's an expensive way to purchase life insurance and a rotten way to make your money grow.

■ Think long and hard before stashing money in your kid's name, because you sacrifice control of the money and you could wreck your family's chances of getting college financial aid. In return, all you get is a modest tax break.

■ Retirement accounts are a great deal. But they aren't without their drawbacks. You lock up the money until age 59½ and you face a fistful of thorny tax issues. With most retirement accounts, however, the benefits outweigh the hassles. But this may not be the case with nondeductible IRAs and variable annuities, so think twice before opening these accounts.

■ Most folks won't leave a bundle to their kids, because they will need every penny saved to finance a retirement that could last 20 or 25 years. If you are determined to enrich your children, you can probably do it, but only if you plan carefully.

That's the end of my 25 myths and my 25 suggested solutions. You don't entirely agree with my new rules for financial success? I couldn't be happier. Nobody on Wall Street has a monopoly on truth. Market strategists don't. Money managers and investment-newsletter writers don't. Brokers, financial planners and insurance agents don't. Newspaper columnists most certainly don't. So treat all financial advice with caution. Look at every investment and every investment strategy with profound skepticism. Think long and hard about every financial myth. If you do that, you will do just fine.

INDEX

account-maintenance fees, 61, 65
Adam Smith's Money World, 97
adjustable-rate mortgages, 176
AFBA Industrial Bank, 165
Against the Gods: The Remarkable Story of Risk (Bernstein), 133
American Association of Retired Persons (AARP), 73
  Investment Program of, 73, 74
American Century Investments, 73, 74, 118, 119, 128
American Stock Exchange, 110
annual renewable term insurance, 201
annuities, 22
  see also variable annuities
asset allocation, 48–53, 97
  age and, 52
  bonds in, 50–51, 97
  cash in, 50–51
  determination of, 52–53
asset-allocation funds, 83–84, 227
automatic investment plans, 18, 33
  investment minimums and, 72–74
automobile insurance, 192

Bacarella, Robert, 87
back-end load, 76

Bacon, Peter W., 35
Baker, David, 86
balanced funds, 82–83, 227
balanced portfolio, 126–35, 228
Bank of New York, 144
Bank Rate Monitor, 177
banks, bank accounts, 41, 67, 102–5, 151
  as bad investments, 104–5
  borrowing from, 158, 160
  money-market funds vs., 105–6, 227
Banz, Rolf W., 37
Barron's, 77, 142
bear markets, 29–30, 44–46, 64–65, 116, 134, 155, 158
Beckwitt, Bob, 87
Beebower, Gilbert L., 50
Bernstein, Peter L., 133–34
bid-ask spread, 60–61, 65
biweekly mortgages, 178
blue-chip stocks, 35, 36, 66, 97
  bid-ask spread of, 60
  in index funds, 98–99
  see also large-company growth-stock funds; large-company value-stock funds; stocks

bond funds, 67, 93, 100, 112–19, 227
  annual expenses of, 112–13
  dividends of, 115
  individual securities vs., 112–14
  junk-, 113, 115
  municipal, 217, 228
  see also specific types of funds
bonds, 108–19
  in asset allocation, 50–51, 97
  in balanced funds, 82–83
  callable, 111–12
  cash investments vs., 103–4
  corporate, 67, 82, 110, 111–12, 113,
    114
  default and, 114
  inflation and, 31, 32, 41, 109,
    118–19, 124–25
  interest rates and, 41, 109–10, 111,
    112–14, 116, 119
  junk, 67, 114
  mortgage, 112
  municipal, 83, 111, 112, 114,
    116–17, 217
  in recessions, 111, 119
  reinvestment risk of, 112–14
  as risky investment, 108–15, 227
  secondary market in, 110, 113
  selling of, 110, 115–16
  taxes and, 107, 111, 116–17
  U.S. government, 33, 45, 67, 82, 106,
    109, 113, 114, 117–19, 124–25
  yields on, 67, 108, 114–16, 117–18
book value, 37
borrowing money, *see* debt; lines of credit
Brinson, Gary P., 50
brokerage firms, 136–37
  account-maintenance fees of, 61, 65
  annual fees of, 139–40
  margin accounts at, 159–60
  see also individual firms
brokers, 16, 136–51, 228
  -client relationship, 138–40
  commissions of, 59–60, 61, 65,
    75–76, 136–37, 139–40, 227
  discount, *see* discount brokers
  full-service, *see* full-service brokers
  load-fund commissions of, 75–76
  real-estate, 185
Bureau of the Public Debt, 113
bypass trusts, 220–21, 223, 224

callable bonds, 111–12
capital-gains tax, 62, 68, 94, 101, 103,
  106, 111, 155, 212–13, 215, 217

*Capital Ideas, The: Improbable Origins of
  Modern Wall Street* (Bernstein),
  133
cash investments, 41, 51, 65, 67, 93,
  103–7, 227
  advantages of, 103
  in asset allocation, 50–51, 97
  bonds vs., 103–4
  as inflation hedge, 104, 124, 125
  -stocks mix in portfolio, 41, 65, 67,
    93, 103, 131–35
cash-value life insurance, 164–65, 193,
  198–202, 222–23, 229
  drawbacks of, 200, 202
  estate taxes and, 199–200, 202,
    222–23
  term insurance vs., 198–99, 200–202
  types of, 199
certificates of deposit, 32, 41, 52, 65,
  67, 103, 104, 105, 151, 227
  see also banks, bank accounts
Certified Financial Planner (CFP),
  150
churning of accounts, 139
collectibles, 41, 121–23, 168
  see also hard assets
college tuition, 17, 19, 52
  extra-mortgage payments and, 207
  gift-tax exclusion and, 210
  home equity and, 207
  IRAs and, 207–8, 209
  savings bonds and, 208
  stock selling for, 130
  see also financial aid
Columbia Funds, 73
Comfin, 68
commercial paper, 105–6, 125
commissions:
  of brokers, 59–60, 61, 65, 75–76,
    136–37, 139–40, 227
  of insurance agents, 200, 202
  of real-estate brokers, 185
commodity futures, 122–23
Community Bankers U.S. Government
  Money Market Fund, 105
compounding of interest, 26–27, 64
conservative investors, 32, 53, 158, 208,
  217
consumer price index (CPI), 118, 124
contrarian strategies, 42
corporate bonds, 67, 82, 110, 111–12,
  113, 114
Craig, James, 87
credit, *see* lines of credit

credit cards, 155, 158
  borrowing against, 165, 228
  low-cost, 165
credit-life insurance, 193
custodial accounts, 74, 203–10
  age of majority and, 204–5
  estate taxes and, 205
  financial aid and, 205–6, 207–10, 229
  investment options in, 206
  taxes on, 204, 207–10

debt, 157–65
  see also lines of credit
Direct Marketing Association, 19
Direct Stock Purchase Plan Clearing-
    house, 144
disability insurance, 191, 195–96
  employer-purchased, self-purchased
    vs., 195
discount brokers, 59–60, 118, 119, 137,
    185, 228
  deep discounters, 142
  on Internet, 142
  list of, 141–42
dividend reinvestment plans, 142, 143
dividend yield, 37
Dodson, Jerome, 87
dollar-cost averaging, 34–35, 44, 65
double-indemnity riders on life
    insurance, 193–94
Dow Jones Industrial Average, 29, 30, 55
dread-disease policies, 194–95
Dreyfus Corporation, 73, 116, 117
DRIP Investor, 144
durable power of attorney, 224

education IRAs, 207–8, 209
  annual contributions to, 208
EE savings bonds, 208
emergency reserve, 16, 19, 151–56, 228
  borrowing money for, 155
  in lifecycle funds, 154–55, 156
  in stock funds, 153–56
  in taxable accounts, 152–56
emerging-market debt fund, 113
emerging-markets stock funds, 39, 77,
    81–82, 88, 89, 90, 93
employer-sponsored retirement plans,
    see 401(k) plans; 403(b) plans;
    retirement-savings plans
equity-income mutual funds, 62
estate planning, 218–25
  bypass trusts, 220–21, 223, 224
  durable power of attorney, 224

gift tax, 221–22
health-care power of attorney, 224
letter of instructions, 224
life insurance policies, see life insur-
    ance
living trusts, 224
living wills, 224
naming of beneficiaries, 223
revocable living trusts, 224
wills, 220, 223, 224
estate taxes, 214, 220–22
  cash-value life insurance and,
    199–200, 202, 222–23
  custodial accounts and, 205
estate-tax exemption, 220–21
expectations of investors, 66–67
extended warranties, 192
extra-mortgage payments, 174–78, 228
  adjustable-rate mortgages and, 176
  college tuition and, 207
  fixed-rate mortgages and, 176–77

Fama, Eugene F., 38
Federal Deposit Insurance Corporation
    (FDIC), 102
Federal Reserve, 113
Fidelity Asset Manager, 87
Fidelity Brokerage Services, 94, 142,
    159
Fidelity Capital Appreciation Fund, 87
Fidelity Investments, 68, 73, 74, 76, 94,
    116, 117
Fidelity Magellan Fund, 85–86
financial aid:
  custodial accounts and, 205–6,
    207–10, 229
  IRAs and, 207–8
"financial-aid planning," 205
Financial Analysts Journal, 50
financial planners, 136, 139, 164, 228
  choosing, 143–50
  meeting with, 150
First Chicago, 144
First Multifund for Daily Income, 105
fixed-rate mortgages, 176–77
flight insurance, 194
Forbes, 70, 77, 86, 153
foreign-bond funds, 113
foreign investments, 206
  developed foreign markets funds,
    38–39, 81–82
  emerging-market debt funds, 113
  emerging-markets stock funds, 39,
    77, 81–82, 88, 89, 90, 93

foreign-bond funds, 113
global funds, 77–81
international funds, 81, 88, *89*
regional funds, 81–82
stocks, 35, 38–39, 65, 66, 77–82, 97, 99
44 Wall Street Fund, 86, 87
Founders Funds, 73, 74
401(k) plans, 21, 22–28, 43, 68, 177, 202
borrowing against, 161–63, 212
rolling over of funds into, 27, 28
withdrawing money from, 27–28, 161
403(b) plans, 21, 22–28, 202
borrowing against, 161–63, 212
withdrawals from, 161
457 plans, 23
French, Kenneth R., 38
front-end load, 76
full-service brokers, 59, 136–40, 228
commissions of, 59–60, 61, 65, 75, 136–37, 139–40
convenience of, 138–39
hand-holding by, 138
funds, *see specific types of funds*
futures, 42
futures contracts, 122

Gabelli, Mario, 87
Gabelli Asset Fund, 87
Gabelli Funds, 73
Garrigan, Richard T., 170
gift-tax exclusion:
educational expenses and, 210, 222
in estate planning, 221–22
medical expenses and, 222
global funds, 77–81, 227
international funds vs., 81–85
see also foreign investments
gold, 41, 120, 125, 168
investment returns on, 122–23
see also hard assets
Goodman, George, 96–97
government bonds, 33, *45*, 67, 82, 106, 109, 113, 114, 117–19, 124–25
Great Crash of stock market (1929), 29
growth stocks, 36
see also large-company growth-stock funds; small-company growth-stock funds
guaranteed investment contract (GIC), 22

hard assets, 41–42, 120–25, 227
inflation and, 41–42, 120–21, 123, 125, 168
as poor investments, 120–22
selling of, 122
trends in, 120–21
Harris Trust, 144
health-care power of attorney, 224
health insurance, 191, 194–95
dread-disease policies, 194–95
hospital-indemnity, 195
Medigap policies, 195
home equity:
borrowing against, 155, 158, 160, 228
college tuition and, 207
in large vs. small houses, 170–71, 228
mortgages and, 169–71
home improvements and repairs, as poor investment, 180–83, 186, 228
trading up vs., 189
home insurance, 187, 191
homes, houses:
buying of, 188–89
capital appreciation in, 186–88
costs of, 16–17, 187, 188
as depreciating asset, 181–82
equity in large vs. small, 170–71
improvements to, 180–83, 189
inflation and value of, 181–82
as investment, 166–71
land value and, 181
repairs to, 180–83, 189
selling stocks for purchase of, 130
trading up of, 184–89
value of, stock values vs., 186
see also real estate
Hood, L. Randolph, 50
hospital-indemnity insurance, 195
HSH Associates, 177

Ibbotson Associates, 29, 44, *45, 46,* 63, 109
IBM, 185–86
imputed rent, 186–87
index funds, 95–101, 135, 227
annual expenses of, 96
capital gains distributions of, 99–100, 217
certainty in, 98
emergency money in, 155
global portfolio of, 99–101, *100*
management of, 95, 101

index funds, *continued*
  performance of, 95–96, 98–99
  S&P 500-stock index vs., 98–99
  tax efficiency of, 101
Individual Retirement Accounts (IRAs),
    21–22, 27, 43, 68, 177, 202
  beneficiaries named in, 214
  college tuition and, 207–8, 209
  drawbacks of, 212–14, 229
  investment minimums in, 73
  nondeductible contributions to, 213,
    214, 215
  opening of, 73
  Roth, 22, 177, 213, 215
  withdrawals from, 161, 163–64,
    212
inflation, 30–32, 97
  bonds and, 31, 32, 41, 109, 118–19,
    124–25
  cash investments as hedge against,
    104, 124, 125
  hard assets and, 41–42, 120–21, 123,
    125, 168
  home values and, 181–82
  real estate and, 167–70
  stocks and, 31–32, 46, 66, 119, 124,
    226
inflation-indexed Treasury bonds:
  as inflation hedge, 118–19, 124–25
  purchasing of, 119
  and stock mix in portfolio, 129–31
inheritance, *see* estate planning
initial public stock offerings (IPOs),
    32
InstantQuote Online Insurance
    Services, 201
Institute of Certified Financial Planners
    (ICFP), 143–50
institutional investors, 105, 110, 122
insurance, 190–202, 229
  disability, 191, 195–96
  extended warranties, 192
  flight, 194
  health, 191, 194–95
  life, *see* life insurance
  long-term care, 196–97
  umbrella liability, 196
insurance agents, 198–202
insurance-quote services, 201
interest, compounding of, 26–27, 64
interest rates, bonds and, 41, 109–10,
    111, 112–14, 116, 119
Internal Revenue Service, 28, 153, 161,
    213

international funds, 88, *89*
  global funds vs., 81
  see also foreign investments
Internet:
  discount brokers on, 142
  financial-planning tools on, 68
  no-load stocks on, 144
  term insurance quote services on,
    201
Invesco Funds Group, 73
investment costs, 59–62, 65, 68, 97,
    227
  account maintenance fees, 61, 65
  brokerage commissions, 59–60, 61,
    65, 75–76, 136–37, 139–40,
    227
investment goals, 97
  planning and, 17–19
  prioritizing of, 15–19
  universal, 16–17
investment minimums of mutual funds,
    70, 72–74
investment portfolio:
  age group and, 52–53, 127
  asset allocation in, 48–53, 97
  balancing of, 42–43, 44, 126–35
  calculating rate of return on, 66–69
  contrarian strategies and, 42
  diversification of stocks in, 35–40,
    44, 51, 65, 75, 93, 100
  foreign stocks in, 35, 38–39, 65, 66,
    77–82, 97, 99
  hard assets in, 41–42, 120–25
  inflation-indexed bond-stock mix in,
    129–31
  no-load stocks in, 142–43
  risk level of, 93
  size of, 89, 89–90
  stocks-cash investments mix in,
    131–35
  taxable vs. retirement accounts in,
    212, 215–17
  zero-coupon bonds-stock mix in,
    128–29
investors:
  conservative, 32, 53, 158, 208, 217
  inconsistency of, 32–33
  lottery ticket mentality of, 48–49
  managing expectations of, 66–67
  risk-tolerance of, 53
IRAs, *see* Individual Retirement
    Accounts
irrevocable life insurance trusts,
    199–200, 222, 224

Jack White & Co., 94, 159
Janus Funds, 73, 74, 87
Jones & Babson, 73, 74
Journal of Finance, 38
Journal of Financial Economics, 37
Journal of Financial Planning, 35
Journal of Investing, 35–40
J. P. Morgan, 144
junk-bond funds, 113, 115
junk bonds, 67, 114
junk mail, 19

Keogh plans, 21, 23, 43, 177
Kiplinger's Personal Finance, 77, 165

large-company growth-stock funds, 36,
    89, 90, 92, 206
large-company value-stock funds, 37,
    88, 89, 92, 206
letter of instructions, 224
level premium term insurance, 201
lifecycle funds, 83–84, 89, 100, 206
    emergency money in, 154–55, 156
    types of, 83
life expectancy in retirement, 27, 46,
    52, 130, 218, 229
life insurance, 191–92
    beneficiaries of, 222, 223
    cash-value, 164–65, 193, 198–202,
        222–23, 229
    credit-, 193
    double-indemnity riders on, 193–94
    in estate planning, 199–200, 222–23,
        224
    term, 193, 198–99, 201
    triple-indemnity riders on, 193–94
limit orders, 61
lines of credit, 158
    cash-value life insurance, 164–65, 228
    credit cards, *see* credit cards
    home-equity, 158, 160, 179, 228
    IRAs, 163–64
    margin accounts, 159–60, 228
    retirement-savings plans and,
        161–63, 228
Lipper Analytical Services, 86
living trusts, 224
living wills, 224
load funds, 75–76, 137
long-term care insurance, 196–97, 219
Lynch, Peter, 85–86

Managing Your Money, 18, 63
margin accounts, 159–60, 228

margin call, 159–60
market, timing of, 55–57, 83, 91, 97
MasterQuote of America, 201
Medicare, 195
Medigap policies, 195
Merrill Lynch & Co., 137
Michigan, University of, 56
Microsoft, 48–49, 51
Microsoft Money, 18, 63
Monetta Fund, 87
Money, 77, 86, 165
money-market mutual funds, 41, 65,
    67, 105–7, 115, 130, 134, 135
    bank accounts vs., 105–6, 227
    choosing of, 106
    emergency reserve in, 152–53, 156
    inflation and, 31, 32, 125
    investments of, 105–6
    and stock mix in portfolio, 128,
        131–35,
    tax-exempt, 106
Morningstar Mutual Funds, 91–92
mortgage bonds, 112
mortgage-interest deduction, 172–78
    as poor tax break, 172–74
mortgages, 17–18, 19, 184
    adjustable-rate, 176
    biweekly, 178
    as enforced savings plan, 170
    extra payments on, *see* extra-
        mortgage payments
    home equity and, 169–71
    inflation and, 168, 173
    paying down of, 174–79, 207
    points, 185
    tax deduction on, *see* mortgage-
        interest deduction
    trading up and, 189
municipal-bond funds, 217, 228
municipal bonds, 83, 111, 112, 114,
    116–17, 217
Mutual Fund Education Alliance, 78
mutual-fund managers, 71, 72, 227
    and index funds, 95, 101
    new stock funds and, 90
    performance of, 88–94
    star, 85–88
    stock-picking skills of, 90–92
    yearly record of, 92
mutual funds, 22
    bonds in, *see* bond funds
    costs of, 58–60, 65, 70–71, 94,
        95–96, 113, 227
    diversification in, 40

mutual funds, *continued*
  individual stocks vs., 39–40, 60, 75
  investment minimums of, 72–74
  load, 75–76, 137
  managers of, *see* mutual-fund managers
  no load, *see* no-load mutual funds
  sector rotation in, 57
  stock, *see* stock funds
  taxes and, 61–62, 68–69, 94
  see also specific types of funds
mutual-fund supermarkets, 94, 142, 159

Nasdaq Stock Market, 110
National Association of Investors Corporation (NAIC), 143
National Association of Personal Financial Advisors (NAPFA), 143–50
NetStock Direct, 144
Neuberger & Berman Management, 73, 74
Nevada, University of, at Las Vegas, 35
Newbould, Gerald D., 35
New York Stock Exchange, 110
1997 tax bill, 21–22, 111, 202, 207, 220
no-load mutual funds, 115, 119, 140, 185
  borrowing against, 159–60
  investment minimums of, 72–74
  list of, 78–81
  load funds vs., 137
  see also bond funds; mutual funds; stock funds
no-load stocks, 142–43
  fees for, 143
  list of, 144–49
nursing-home insurance, *see* long-term care insurance

options, 42

Pagliari, Joseph L., Jr., 170
Parnassus Fund, 87
Pennsylvania, University of, Wharton School at, 66
Pennsylvania Mutual Fund, 87
pensions, traditional, 20–21
  employee-run plans vs., 21, 27
  employer-sponsored retirement savings plans vs., 25
  see also retirement accounts; retirement savings plans
permanent insurance, *see* cash-value life insurance

personal-finance software, 18, 63, 68, 177
planning, investment goals and, 17–19
points, mortgage, 185
Poon, Percy S., 35
portfolio, *see* investment portfolio
power of attorney, 224
price-earnings (P/E) ratio, 36
probate, 214, 224
  avoiding, 223
profit-sharing plans, 22
prospectuses, 77

Quicken, 18, 63
Quicken Financial Network, 68
QuickQuote Insurance Agency, 201
Quotesmith Corporation, 201

real estate, 41, 123, 181
  inflation and, 167–70
real-estate brokers, 185
real-estate investment trusts, 123
Real Estate Review, 170
rebalancing, 42–43, 44
  of stock portfolio, 43
  of taxable accounts, 43
recessions, bonds in, 111, 119, 124
regional funds, 81–82, 227
reinvestment risks of bonds, 112–14
Remodeling, 182, 183
rent, imputed, 186–87
retirement:
  balanced portfolio goals and, 126–35
  early, 27
  income in, 17, 18–19, 46, 52–53
  life expectancy in, 27, 46, 52, 130, 218, 229
  portfolio funds withdrawn for, 130–31
  stock sales for income in, 130–31
  see also Individual Retirement Accounts; retirement accounts; retirement-savings plans
retirement accounts, 18, 33
  beneficiaries of, 213–14, 223
  capital gains and, 212–13, 215
  fees of, 61
  investment minimums for, 73
  taxable accounts as alternative to, 215–17
  taxes and, 26, 61–62, 68, 94, 101, 161, 163–64, 212
  trading activity in, 62, 94, 127
  variable annuities vs., 216

see also investment portfolio; retirement-savings plans; Individual Retirement Accounts
retirement-savings plans, employer-sponsored, 21–28, 212–13, 214–15, 226
  borrowing against, 161–63, 228
  compounding in, 26–27
  employer-matched funds in, 26
  nondeductible contributions to, 162
  pretax contributions to, 25–27
  rebalancing in, 43
  traditional pensions vs. employee-run, 21, 27
  withdrawals from, 161
  see also 401(k) plans; 403(b) plans
revocable living trusts, 224
risk-reduction strategies:
  bonds and, 41
  cash investments and, 41
  contrarian strategies, 42
  diversifying stocks, 35–40
  dollar-cost averaging, 34–35
  hard assets and, 41–42
  rebalancing and, 42–43
Roth IRA, 22, 177, 213, 215
round lots, in stocks, 186
Royce, Charles, 87

S&P 500 funds, 98–99
  see also index funds
savings accounts, *see* banks, bank accounts
savings bonds, 208
Savings Incentive Match Plan for Employees (SIMPLE), 23
savings strategies, 17–18
Schwab (Charles) Corporation, 73, 74, 94, 99–100, 101, 142, 159, 216
Scudder Funds, 73
sector funds, 57, 72, 82, 227
sector rotation, 57, 91, 97
Securities and Exchange Commission (SEC), 76
SelectQuote Insurance Services, 201
SEP (Simplified Employee Pension) plans, 21, 23
Series EE savings bonds, 208
Seyhun, H. Nejat, 56
short selling, 42
short-term bond funds, 107, 114, 116, 130, 135, 188, 228
  emergency reserve in, 152–53, 156

short-term municipal-bond funds, 116–17, 135
Siegel, Jeremy J., 66
SIMPLE (Savings Incentive Match Plan for Employees), 23
Simplified Employee Pension (SEP) plans, 21, 23
small-company growth-stock funds, 37–38, 77, 88, *89,* 92, 97, 206
small-company value-stock funds, 38, 77, 88, *89,* 90, 92, 94, 97, 206
Smart Money, 86
Smith Barney, 137
Social Security, 24, 152, 226
  disability benefits of, 195
software, personal-finance, 18, 63, 68, 177
spread, bid-ask, 60–61, 65
Standard & Poor's 500-stock index, 30, 44, 55, 63, 65, 87, 135, 154, 155
  index funds vs., 98–99
  performance of, *45*
Stein Roe Mutual Funds, 73, 74
stock funds, 36–40, 65, 70–101, 135, 206
  annual expenses of, 76–77, 96
  choosing of, 74–84
  costs of, 58–60, 65, 75–77
  emergency reserve in, 153–56
  emerging-markets, 39, 77, 81–82, 88, *89,* 90, 93
  failed promises of, 72–75
  foreign, *see* foreign investments
  high-minimum, 77
  investment minimums of, 70, 72–74
  list of, 78–81
  load, 75–76, 137
  managers of, 85–94, 95
  no-load, 60, 72–74
  performance of, 72, 85–94
  types of, 77–84
  unloading of, 93–94
  unwieldy growth of, 92
  see also investment portfolio; mutual funds
stock market, 54–62
  downturns in, 29–30, 44–46, 64–65, 158
  global, 38–39
  Great Crash (1929), 29, 155
  1973–74 crash of, 64–65, 134, 155
  1987 crash of, 29, 72

stock market, *continued*
    sectors of, 57, 82, 91
    stock selection in outpacing of,
        57–58
    timing of, 55–57, 83, 91, 97
    volatility of, 55–56
stocks:
    ask price of, 60–61
    in asset allocation, 48–53, 97
    in balanced funds, 82–83
    bid price of, 60–61
    blue-chip, *see* blue-chip stocks
    brokerage commissions on, 59–60,
        61, 75, 136–37, 139–40
    capital appreciation of, 212–13
    and cash investments mix in portfo-
        lio, 131–35
    costs of, 59–62
    currency swings and, 38–40
    diversification of, 35–40, 44, 51, 65,
        75, 93, 100
    dollar-cost averaging in, 34–35, 44
    foreign, 35, 38–39, 65, 66, 77–82, 97,
        99
    growth, 36, 37–38
    inflation and, 31–32, 46, 66, 119,
        124, 226
    and inflation-indexed bonds mix in
        portfolio, 129–31
    on Internet, 60
    as lifetime investment, 46–47
    and market timing, 55–57, 83, 91, 97
    mutual funds vs. individual, 39–40,
        60, 75
    no-load, 142–43, 144–49
    purchase of, 136–50
    rate of return on, 63–69
    in retirement-savings plans, 18, 22,
        52–53
    risk level of, 30–48
    in round lots, 186
    value, 37, 38
    and zero-coupon bonds mix in port-
        folio, 128–29, 228
stocks, selling of:
    for college tuition, 130
    expenses in, *see* commissions, of
        brokers
    for home purchase, 130
    for retirement income, 130–31
Stocks for the Long Run (Siegel), 66
Strong Funds, 73, 74
style rotation, *see* sector rotation
Sweeney, Tom, 87

tactical asset allocators, 83
taxable accounts, 62, 68–69
    emergency money in, 152–56
    index funds in, 101
    rebalancing in, 43
    as retirement account alternative,
        212, 215–17
tax deductions, 174
tax-deferred accounts, *see* retirement
        accounts; retirement-savings plans
taxes, 97, 104
    on bond income, 107, 111, 116–17
    cash-value life insurance and, 199
    on custodial accounts, 204, 207–10
    estate, *see* estate taxes
    as investment cost, 61–62
    on mutual funds, 61–62
    on retirement accounts, 26, 61–62,
        68, 94, 101, 161, 163–64, 212
Temper of the Times Communications,
        143
term insurance, 193
    cash-value life insurance vs., 198–99,
        200–202
    premiums of, 199, 200
    quote services for, 201
    types of, 201
TermQuote, 201
timing of market, 55–57, 83, 91, 97
total return, 116, 186
Towneley Capital Management, 56
trading up of homes, 184–89, 228–29
    capital appreciation in, 186–88
    expenses of, 185–86
    mortgages and, 189
Treasury bills, 41, 106, 125
    performance of, *46*
Treasury bonds, 33, 113, 114, 117–19,
        124–25
    direct purchase of, 113
    inflation-indexed, *see* inflation-
        indexed Treasury bonds
    performance of, *45*
    yield of, 67
triple-indemnity riders on life insur-
        ance, 193–94
T. Rowe Price Associates, 68, 73, 74,
        94, 117
trusts, 204
    bypass, 220–21, 223, 224
    irrevocable life insurance, 199–200,
        222, 224
    living, 224
12b-1 fee, 76

umbrella liability insurance, 192, 196
unified credit, 220–21
unified credit-shelter trust, 221
Uniform Gifts to Minors Act (UGMA), 204
Uniform Transfers to Minors Act (UTMA), 204
USAA Federal Savings Bank, 165
USAA Investment Management, 73, 74, 116, 117
USAA Life Insurance Co., 201
utilities, 62

value stocks:
    performance of, 37
    risk and reward of, 38
    see also large-company value-stock funds; small-company value-stock funds
Vanguard Group, 68, 73, 74, 94, 98, 99, 100–101, 113, 116, 117, 216

variable annuities, 211–17
    buying of, for children, 216
    capital gains and, 212–13, 215
    drawbacks of, 215, 216, 229
variable life insurance, 199

Wall Street Journal, 16, 71, 82, 142, 153, 165, 175
    mutual-fund survey of, 77
Warburg Pincus Funds, 73, 74
Williams, Richard E., 35
wills, 220, 223, 224
    living, 224, 225
Wright State University, 35

zero-coupon bond funds, 118, 119, 128
zero-coupon bonds, 135
    long-term investing in, 117–18
    purchasing of, 118
    and stock mix in portfolio, 128–29, 228
    taxes and, 117

ABOUT THE AUTHOR

JONATHAN CLEMENTS is an award-winning financial journalist. Born in London, England, and educated at Cambridge University, he spent more than three years at *Forbes* magazine in New York before moving to *The Wall Street Journal* in January 1990. During his eight years at the *Journal,* he has spearheaded the paper's mutual-funds coverage, written the "Heard on the Street" column and authored personal-finance articles, before being given his own column in October 1994. The "Getting Going" column appears every Tuesday in the *Journal.*

Clements is also the author of *Funding Your Future: The Only Guide to Mutual Funds You'll Ever Need,* published in 1993. He won the 1996 "Articles of Excellence" award from the Certified Financial Planner Board of Standards, the 1992 American University/ICI Education Foundation award for personal-finance writing, and the New York State Society of Certified Public Accountants' 1988 award for excellence in financial writing.

Clements works at the *Journal's* headquarters in New York City and lives in Metuchen, New Jersey.